A LAYMAN'S VIEW OF SOME
(ROUGH NO
BY W. J. PO
TYPED SEPTEMBER 1977

Wilfred James Joseph Power was born in Duke Street, Devonport, as the third child of James Joseph Power and Emily Rose Ellen Power on 23rd February 1909.
Wilfred won an apprenticeship as an Electrical Fitter in the Devonport Naval Dockyard eventually living in Beaconsfield Road, Plymouth. He died in 1992 aged 83 years.
Wilfred compiled most of this book during the 1950's and 60's eventually typing it into an octavo manuscript form in 1977. The only churches included are those in the pre-1967 Plymouth boundary area and do not include Plympton and Plymstock. Only two copies of the book – the original and a carbon copy – are thought to have been made and this version digitally transcribed from the original book (photo below) is reproduced in his memory. G.K.B – 2015

A LAYMAN'S VIEW INDEX

Church of England

Church of St. Aidan, Ernesettle	8
Church of St. Andrew, Plymouth	8
The Abbey Hall	11
The Prysten House	11
The Church of All Saints, Harwell Street	12
Church of St. Anne, Swilly	13
Church of the Ascension, Crownhill	13
Church of St. Aubyn, Devonport	14
The Church of St. Augustine	14
Church of St. Barnabas, Wilton Street	16
The Church of St. Bartholomew, Milehouse	16
Parish Church of St. Boniface, St. Budeaux	18
Parish Church of St. Budeaux	18
Church of St. Catherine, Lockyer Street	19
Church of St. Chad, Whitleigh	20
Charles Church	21
Household of the Faith	24
Christ Church, Eton Place	25
The Church of St. Edward the Martyr, Eggbuckland	26
Parish Church of Emmanuel	27
Church of St. Francis, Honicknowle	29
The Parish Church of St. Gabriel	29
The Church of St. George, East Stonehouse	31
Parish of Southway, Church of the Holy Spirit	32
Church of Holy Trinity, Southside Street	32
Parish Church of St. James the Less, Millbay	33
Church of St. James the Less, Ham	34
Church of St. James the Great, Devonport	36
Church of St. John the Baptist, Duke St., Devonport	37
St. John the Evangelist, Sutton on Plym	37
Church of St. Jude	38

Chapel of St Katherine, Citadel	40
Church of St. Lo, Devonport Dockyard	41
Church of St. Luke, Richmond Walk	41
Church of St. Luke, Plymouth	42
Church of St. Mark, Ford	43
Church of St. Martin, Peverell	44
Church of St. Mary Magdalene, Alvington Street	44
Church of St. Mary, James Street, Devonport	45
Parish Church of St. Mary, Tamerton	46
St. Mary the Virgin, Laira	47
Church of St. Matthew, Stonehouse	48
Church of St. Mathias	48
St. Mathias Mission Church	50
Church of St. Michael, Albert Road, Devonport	50
Church of St. Michael, West Hoe	51
The Military Chapel, Devonport	51
Church of St. Nicholas, R.N. Barracks	52
Parish Church of St. Pancras	52
Parish Church of St. Paul, Stonehouse	54
Parish of Emmanuel, Church of St. Paul, Efford	56
The Church of St. Paul, Morice Square, Devonport	56
Church of St. Peter, Wyndham Square	57
Mission Church of St. Philip and St. James, Weston Mill	59
The Church of St. Philip, Weston Mill	60
Church of St. Saviour	61
Church of St. Simon	62
Church of St. Stephen, George Street, Devonport	62
Parish Church of Stoke Damerel	63
Church of St. Thomas the Apostle, Keyham	68
Mission of St. Thomas	69

Non Conformist

Non Conformist Churches, General	
Crownhill Baptist Church	70

Efford Baptist Church 71
Emmanuel Baptist Church, North Road, Plymouth 71
Estover Baptist Church 72
Ford Baptist Church 73
George Street Baptist 74
Hope Baptist Church 76
Morice Baptist Church 77
Mutley Baptist Church 78
Pembroke Street Baptist Church 79
Salisbury Road Baptist Church 81
St. Budeaux Baptist Church 82
Other Baptist Places of Worship 82

Methodists Churches

Compton Methodist Church 83
Devonport Methodist Central Hall 83
Plymouth Methodist Central Hall 84
Ford Methodist Church 86
Greenbank Methodist Church 87
Ker Street Wesleyan Methodist Chapel, Devonport 88
King Street Methodist Church 89
Mutley Methodist Church 90
Pennycross Methodist Church 91
Whitleigh Methodist Church 93
Stonehouse Methodist Mission 94
(formerly Stonehouse Wesleyan M.C)
Crownhill Methodist Church 95
St. Levan Road Methodist Church, Stuart Road 96
St. Budeaux Methodist Church, Victoria Road 97
Peverell Methodist Church 97
Wesleyan Methodist Chapel, Ebrington Street 98
Keyham Methodist Church 98
Cobourg Street Primitive Methodist Church 99
Methodist Chapel in Gloucester Street, Morice Town 100

Albert Road Methodist Church	100
Mount Gould Methodist Church	100
Millbridge Methodist Church	100
St. George's Road Methodist Church	101
Belmont Methodist Church, Stoke	101
Embankment Road Methodist Church	101
Tamerton Methodist Church	101
Ernesettle Methodist Church	102
Halcyon Road Methodist Church	103
Zion Methodist Church, The Hoe, Plymouth	103
Laira Methodist Church, now renamed Zion Methodist	104

Roman Catholic

Church of Christ the King, The Hoe, Plymouth	105
Church of the Holy Redeemer, Keyham	106
The Church of the Holy Family, Beacon Park	106
Holy Cross	107
Our Lady of Mount Carmel, Efford	108
Church of St. Edward the Confessor, Holland Road, Peverell	108
The Cathedral of St. Mary and St. Boniface, Wyndham Street	109
Church of St. Michael and Joseph, James Street, Devonport	111
Church of St. Paul, St. Budeaux	111
Church of St. Peter, Crownhill	112
Church of St. Thomas More, Bamfylde Way, Southway	113

United Reformed

Derriford United Reformed Church	113
Laira United Reformed Church	114
Pilgrim United Reformed Church, St. Levan Road	115
Sherwell United Reformed Church	117

Wycliffe Church, Albert Road	120
Honicknowle United Reformed Church	121
Western College Congregational Chapel	122
Batter Street Congregational Church	122
Congregational General Notes	122
Western College	123

Other Denominations

The Seventh Day Adventist Church	123
Jehovah Witness	124
Plymouth Spiritualist Churches	124

General 125

The Apostolic Church, Gordon Terrace	126
The Bethel Mission, Barbican	128
The Brethren (Plymouth Brethren)	129
Church of Christ, Scientist	132
The Christadelphian Ecclesia, Portland Villas, Plymouth	133
The Elim Church, Notte Street	134
Plymouth Friends (Quakers)	135
The Church of Jesus Christ of the Latter Day Saints (Mormons)	136
The Salvation Army	138
The Seventh Day Adventist Church	140
The Synagogue, Catherine Street	140
Unitarian Church, Plymouth	142
Unitarian Church in Devonport	144
Devonport Town Mission, Granby Street (Zion)	145
Lower Street Mission	148
The Moravian Chapel, James Street, Devonport	148
The Hydesville Institute	149
Zoar Mission, Devonport	149

A LAYMAN'S VIEW OF SOME PLYMOUTH CHURCHES

Foreword

These notes have been titled 'A Layman's View of some Plymouth Churches'. The word 'church' has been used in its widest sense, that of a meeting place for religious observance. This is not intended to be a history but just a 'view'.

I have tried to include every denomination but it has not been found reasonable to cover every church. As far as is known no comprehensive survey of Plymouth churches exists and it is felt that many details (often those just in the memory of older people) may be forgotten and lost forever if not now recorded.

In making these notes, errors are sure to have crept in, despite efforts to make the account as accurate as possible it has been found that sometimes the records used for reference do not agree, and people's memories (including my own) can be misleading. However, it is felt that inclusion of any miss-statements I hope there are not too many, may be justified as if I had been afraid of making a mistake, I could not have made these notes.

Church history in Plymouth has seen many changes - from the days of intolerance to the present period when it seems that differing denominations are moving closer together. We see R.C's using a C of E pulpit, and co-operation between Baptists and Methodists. All this must be good. When searching for material for this account, a remark was made to me "God has many names but there is only one God".

W. J. Power. 1977

CHURCH OF ENGLAND

Church of St. Aidan, Ernesettle.

As early as 1482 a chapel existed at Ernesettle so that baptisms and burials could take place there instead of the distant St. Andrews. Owing to the recent growth of the district and the need for a place of worship in the area services were begun in private houses in 1949 and later a Sunday School was opened. A parish was created from that of St. Budeaux and a priest licensed in 1951, a foundation stone being laid for the Church and Hall in 1953. The completed buildings were opened in 1954. The Church was dedicated by the Bishop of Exeter, who also performed the consecration ceremony in 1959. A gale in 1965 caused severe damage, the copper roof being ripped off. This is a red brick structure facing Ernesettle Green. It has a small tower surmounted by a slender cross and containing one bell.

The Church of St. Andrew, Plymouth.

The oldest part of the present building dates from the late 14th century. It is certain that a church existed before this on the site, one being mentioned in 1291, in a Survey ordered by Pope Nicholas and we even have the name of a priest attached to the church in 1087. In 1385 a south aisle was added and in one year a north aisle. 20 years or so later the tower was built.
In the early 19th century the church appears to have become over crowded with furniture - a forest of pews is mentioned and the report goes on to say the pews were 'high and snug, fit for sitting and perhaps for sleeping but unfit for anything else'. It was decided in 1818 to divide the building into two churches and to this end plans were drawn up by a Torpoint architect. Later, however, this decision was changed and John Foulston was called in to make less drastic internal re-arrangements. Later comments were that he cleared away too much, but being the great architect that he was he

probably did very efficiently what he had been asked to do. It is assumed that it was at this time that the three deck pulpit was removed, then again restored in 1874.

The galleries were taken away. Much of the valuable glass which had been destroyed at the time of the Reformation was replaced, a pre-1939/45 war description states that the building was in the perpendicular style and consisted of a chancel and nave, with aisles extending the whole length. Mentioned also are transepts, north and south porches, an embattled western tower with pinnacles built about 1460, a clock and a peal of ten bells, seven of which were cast in 1749. Bells where re-hung in 1897. Bells by Thomas Bilbie. Two marked: 'Thomas Bilbie cast us all. Thomas Bilbie cast all wee'. The description continues by stating that the aisles were separated from the nave and chancel by a series of pointed arches springing from clustered shafts with carved foliated capitals; the eastern portions of the aisles forming chapels. Under the chancel was a crypt said to communicate with an ancient building to the south west of the church called the Prysten House. Building was restored 1874/75 under the direction of Sir Gilbert Scott, F.S.A. Organ built by James Parsons in 1737.

Total length of building 185 feet. 1,800 sittings. This pre-war description concludes by noting that the Register dates from 1581 and contains the names of great seamen such as Hawkins, Frobisher and Drake as well as other great men of the Elizabethan age.

The Churchwarden's accounts are of some interest; entries such as '1635: Ye Clerke Gyles was paid 10 shillings for keeping out ye dogges and keeping in ye boyes' suggest that neither 'dogges' nor 'boyes' have changed much.

The graveyard which had existed for many years in front of the church later became an embarrassment as the level of the ground had risen above that of the surrounding road. About 1894 the remains of those buried there were removed to a new site at Westwell Gardens and a small park created instead. This consisted of four paths laid out in the shape of the cross of St. Andrew, at the central point of which was a monument containing statues. The monument (which had been designed by James Hine, an architect of some note) was to commemorate those who had previously been interred in that place.

Perhaps the biggest change possible to the Church of St. Andrew in its long history came when the town was blitzed in 1941. The church was gutted and nothing but the walls and tower left standing. Almost immediately the word 'RESURGAM' appeared over the north entrance, flowers were planted inside the walls and the building became known as 'The Garden Church', some services being held amid the ruins.

In 1949 H.M. The Queen, then Princess Elizabeth, laid a stone to commemorate the start of reconstruction. This took about eight years, the church being reopened and re-consecrated in 1957.

In the interval period, nearby St. Catherine's became the temporary Mother Church of Plymouth. On the opening of the re-constructed St. Andrews, the church of St.Catherine was closed and later demolished in the interests of town planning, the site now being used as a car park for the new Council House. To come to the present time: The Church of St. Andrew has much of interest. Of some note is the 'Drake Scratching'. The history of this is not known but it is thought to have been done by a workman carrying out repairs in the 16th century, when Drake brought fame to the country and to Plymouth by his circumnavigation of the globe. Scratching, probably executed 1580/1590, can be seen on the window ledge on the south side, almost opposite the Royal Parade entrance. The font, too, is worth mentioning. Made in 1661, it was replaced by a newer one 1875. The 1661 font was found in the garden of a local resident, doing duty as a birdbath. Presented to the Church, it was used at St. Catherine's until the closing stages of reconstruction, when it was reinstalled at St. Andrew's to replace the Victorian font destroyed in the bombing.

The monument which had stood in front of the church was damaged during the war and considered unsafe. We assume it was broken up but we do know that two statues were retained and these have now been built into the wall of the Guildhall. It is nice to think that at least part of the monument remains.

The present building still retains its air of attractive dignity. Much modern stained glass has been fitted, one window of particular note being the Astor window at the rear of the church under the tower. It is fitting that it overlooks the City Centre, the Astor's having contributed so much to the wellbeing of Plymouth.

The Abbey Hall

Behind the church was a building known as the Abbey. It must have had a close connection with St. Andrew's but no details are available. In 1920 it was being used as a factory but it was purchased and restored, now being known as the Abbey Hall. Stone was laid by the Bishop of Bradford in 1923, the restored building was completed in 1925 as a memorial to those who lost their lives in the War. One of the few halls available after the devastation of the City Centre during the 1939/45 war, it was much used at this period and continues to give valuable service.

The Prysten House.

Built in the 15th century it was obviously used as a priests' house - the monks from Plympton Priory who served St. Andrew's Church at this time probably used it. After the dissolution of the monasteries in 1539 it passed to secular ownership, and after having many uses, was bought back by St. Andrew's and carefully restored 1920/1930. It stands in Finewell Street and inside the building is a well - probably the 'fine well' from which the street got its name. Built round a central courtyard, the building has many interesting features.

During the American War of Independence in 1813, the British H.N.5. Felican was in action with the U.S.N. Brig. Argus.

During the fighting, the Captain, William Henry Allen and a midshipman, were killed. Their bodies were brought ashore and buried in the churchyard with expressions of respect and regret. A memorial stone was placed behind the church inscribed 'Here sleep the brave'.

During the restoration of the Prysten House the stone was recalled and the American 'Daughters of 1812' provided for the restoration of the doorway leading into the house to commemorate the chivalrous act of so many years ago. The doorway has been aptly named the 'Door of Unity' with the original memorial stone now mounted alongside. A service is held here each year, normally attended by a representative from the American Embassy. It is good to think that the close ties which we have with the Americans (so many of whom gave their lives in support of this country and for the cause of freedom during the late war) are kept alive by ceremonies such as this, close ties which, it is hoped, will continue.

The Church of All Saints, Harwell St.

In 1875 the Parish of All Saints was created from that of St. Peter in Wyndham Square.

The building was started in 1873 to the design of James Hine, but was not really completed until 1910. Erected on what was formerly a market garden it was sometimes known as "The Garden Church" because of this association.

A pre-war description states it to be limestone in the Early English style, consisting of chancel, nave, aisles, and western porch, 400 sittings. A clergy house was erected in 1887 and in1892 a parish room, provision for Sunday school, and four class rooms were added.

Due to town planning, the church is no longer amid a populous district and the Parish has now merged with that of St. Peter, from which Church it is now served, having no resident priest of its own.

Church of St. Anne, Swilly.

In 1930 a temporary wooden church, that of St. Anne, was built in the Swilly area to serve that district and the growing Ham Estate. It was a daughter church of St. Mark in Ford.
When the new church of St. James the Less was erected in Ham Drive, the church of St. Anne became redundant and was demolished.
A block of flats has now been built on the site.

Church of the Ascension, Crownhill.

In 1842 Trinity Church was built and, although no longer used as a church, it still stands in Budshead Road. In 1941 it was used as an Air Raid Post.
Trinity Church was replaced by the Church of the Ascension, an impressive modern building, which, together with the vicarage, stands at the top of Manadon Hill. It was erected in 1956. Internally it is an unusual church with the altar being brought forward towards the congregation a beautifully decorated canopy supported on slim pillars is over the altar, behind which is a wall carrying twelve windows. These were conceived by Geoffrey Clarke, the colours in them being used symbolically:-

Blue, the predominant colour to remind of the presence of Jesus Christ, the Son of God.

Amber, symbolising Nan, the child of God's love.

Green and Red, denoting the forces of evil and disunity threatening Man's communion with his Creator.

The church has a maroon coloured roof held up by slender granite pillars, white painted pews.

The interior gives the impression of spaciousness and light. Despite its modernity it appears dignified and to embody all the best of present day design.

Church of St. Aubyn, Devonport.

Erected in 1772 as a chapel-of-ease to Stoke Damerel, the chancel being added in 1885.

Originally described as of substantial and plain appearance with octagonal spire above a Doric portico the interior fitted with galleries on three sides supported by stone pillars. It has three aisles and a chancel has been added. This is not quite accurate today as the porch has been removed (possibly owing to road widening) and the spire truncated. This does not improve the appearance of the church although the tower below the shortened spire does contain a clock.

The interior of the church is probably much the same as it was 200 years ago. Erected as a Garrison Chapel it has served and continues to serve the needs of the area.

It was built by Piers St. Aubyn who was responsible for several churches in the Devonport area.

The Church of St. Augustine.

The foundation stone was laid in 1899 on a site previously known as 'Withy Pool'. In digging the foundations for one of the main pillars it was necessary to go down 43 feet before rock could be found.

The partly finished building (originally known as the Church of St. Mark, but changed to avoid confusion with St. Mark's in Ford) was consecrated in 1904 by the Bishop of Exeter. The crypt had been opened in 1900. Work went ahead, the building having granite pillars and a roof of pitch pine, but due to lack of funds the fabric of the church was incomplete, so as a temporary measure the west end was enclosed in wood.

A bell from the cruiser 'Volage', built at Blackwell in 1869, was bought in 1904.

Furnishing of the church went on by the installation of a pulpit, pews, choir stalls etc. some of these items being given by local contractors. In 1914 there was a serious fire in the incomplete wooden portion.

The present vicarage was bought in 1919 for £750.

The church itself was not complete until 1933 when two bays and a choir vestry on the North West side had been added. Said to be in the Gothic style, it seated 700.

And so to June 1943 when the building was almost completely destroyed in the blitz. A service was held in the ruins the morning after the damage, and later at the nearby Beechwood factory. Services were also shared with those of St. Matthias. Later again, after much hard work by willing workers, the crypt could be used again, although when it rained water poured down from the unroofed floor of the church above. It says much for those using the crypt, faced as they were with water from above and the flooding which took place at high tide due to the low lying position in Lipson Vale.

The rebuilding of the church went on but it was not until October 1954 (50 years from the date of its original consecration) that it was reopened for worship. The only items from the old church to have escaped destruction were one of the pews and the brass lectern. The marble from the chancel, some of the figures on the choir stalls and some of the choir stall ends also exist.

The present organ and carved screen came from Christ Church (closed and demolished in 1966) in Eton Place.

This is a fine church whose congregation showed so much courage and determination during the war years. The carvings on the Lady Altar are outstanding. They were executed by Miss Violet Pinwell and portray various items of A.R.P. equipment such as a stirrup pump, respirator, rattle and tinhat - an unusual and original way to commemorate the work done by members of the A.R.P. during the blitz.

Church of St. Barnabas, Wilton St.

The first part of this church was built in 1881 as a chapel-of-ease to Stoke Damerel, the architect being J. Piers St. Aubyn. The building was completed in 1894 and became a Parish Church in its own right in 1904.
An iron building which had served as a Parish Hall was removed to Forest Avenue at Peverell in 1908 to become Pennycross Methodist Church, and the present permanent Hall erected at a cost of £1,550. (Architect: C. Cheverton). The organ from Church of St. Matthew, Stonehouse.

The Church of St. Bartholomew, Milehouse.

Built on the site of the home of Robert Falcon Scott, it is a very modern structure, resembling in some ways the Church of the Ascension at Crownhill. But for the beginning we have to go back to the year 1881.
For some time Devonport had been growing outwards and for many people the church at Stoke Damerel was becoming increasingly remote. To satisfy the needs of a growing area, the Higher Stoke Mission Chapel to seat 100 was opened in Church Street on the site now occupied by a school, the Mission being of course, a daughter of Stoke Damerel.
In 1904 we hear of three churches in the area; Stoke Damerel, St. Barnabas and St. Bartholomew - the first time we know of its being referred to as a church.
In the early 1920s much building was going on in the Swilly and Milehouse areas and the need for another church to serve this expansion became apparent. Consequently, a new Church of St. Bartholomew - a wooden shed like structure - was made in Browning Road, Milehouse.
The seating, bell and organ came from the Church Street premises and the new building seated 250.

It was realised in 1938 that as Milehouse was becoming the geographical centre of the City it was time to consider the building of a larger and more permanent church, but when the war broke out in 1939 ideas had to be shelved and the services continued at Browning Road. This went on until 1941 when the wooden church was badly damaged in the blitz. Services were held for a time in the crypt of St. Mary's in Collingwood Road (St. Mary's now demolished - see Stoke Damerel) and later in a hut adjoining the church, which although damaged had been repaired to enable it to be used.

In 1951 repairs had been carried out to the wooden church and it was used again.

It was time to implement some of the 1938 plans and, to this end, ground at Outlands was purchased. This site itself is of some historic significance, having been once the home of Scott of the Antarctic. Later, it was let to J.B.Love, the proprietor of a large drapery establishment in Catherine St., Devonport ('Jimmy' Love to the older people). The house was badly damaged during the war and later demolished.

In 1944 the site was purchased and in 1948 an adjoining field was also obtained. It was not until 1958, however, that the foundation stone for the new church was laid. The building was completed and consecrated towards the end of 1959. (Architect: Mr. Luxton. Contractors: Messrs. Gilbert and Coles). Oddly enough, on the same day the Pilgrim United Reformed Church in St. Levan Road was opened and a close association has always existed between the two churches.

As was noted at the beginning of these details, this is a modern church of attractive appearance internally and externally, having a clean uncluttered aspect. Its connection with Robert Falcon Scott is commemorated by a plaque on the entrance, and in the vestry is a piece of tree on which he had carved his name. Another link with the past is that the organ installed in the church came from the bombed St. Mary's, formerly in James Street, Devonport.

Parish Church of St. Boniface, St. Budeaux.

As the need for a church in the lower part of St. Budeaux became apparent as in 1895 services were being held in a room over a stable in Yeoman's Terrace. Later, services were being conducted in the Masonic Hall in Victoria Road.
A Mission Hall was erected to seat 340 persons in 1901 and dedicated to St. Boniface, and this served until 1913 when the present church was built and consecrated. The Parish was formed in 1933.
The 1913 building still remains but has been greatly extended by the addition of a very modern structure at the west end.
From St. Budeaux Square the appearance of the lower part of Victoria Road is greatly enhanced by the placing of this attractively modernised church. The architect for the original building was Mr. W.D. Caroe.
Some pews from demolished Church of St. Matthew, Stonehouse.

The Parish Church of St. Budeaux.

In 480 a Celtic saint, St. Budoc, came to Budshead. In 1482 Bishop Courtenay of Exeter responded to an appeal from the 'Chapelry' of St. Budeaux that baptisms and burials should take place in their Chapel rather than in the distant church of St. Andrew. This was reasonable because to get to St. Andrew's would have been quite a journey in those days, the route going through Weston Mill by ill kept roads. It is thought that the Chapel was at Lower Ernesettle and it was not until 1563 that the present church was built, probably through the generosity of Roger Budockshead of Budockshead Manor, who also provided a piece of ground to the north east of the church. Rent for this ground was one penny a year and it was considered lawful for parishioners to 'play honest games' there except during divine service.
The new church (1563) occupies a fine position with wonderful views, and despite the building in the vicinity, is still a local

landmark. The pillars inside the church are of some note. Made of granite which is quite normal but the unusual feature is that the capital on one pillar is different from those on the others. It is believed that this may have come from the earlier church, as did the granite font.

Church has a square tower with six bells. Again, it is almost certain that three of these came from the previous building and are thus older than the church itself. Many interesting monuments can be seen; perhaps the most outstanding of these is the Gorges Memorial. Of considerable note, too, is the Register which records the marriage of Sir Francis Drake to Mary Newman in 1569. Mary Drake was also buried here.

The sundial over the south door, erected in 1670, bears the inscription in Latin: 'On this moment is eternity suspended'. The churchwardens accounts note: 'Paid for dyall...£1.17.8d' 'lime and fetching dyall....1.6d' and these expenses seem to have been completed by 'beer for workmen....6d'.

Outside the church by the porch is a very old stone representing a cross within a circle. The History of this is not definitely known but it is almost certain that it formed part of the pediment over the doorway of the previous building.

The Parish Church of St. Budeaux is one of the oldest and most historic in the City. It is certainly worth a visit. There is so much interest that it is fortunate that an excellent booklet is available at the Church giving detailed description of its past.

Church of St. Catherine, Lockyer Street.

Originally a chapel-of-ease to St. Andrew's it was erected in 1823 to the design of John Foulston and known as St. Andrew's Chapel. The foundation stone was laid by Rev. Robert Lampen.

A pre-war description of the building described it as 'plain....of stone and granite in the Basilican style and consists of a chancel, nave, with a belfry surmounted by a cross and containing one bell.

Restored 1879/80. Choir vestry added in 1907. Roof renewed 1912, 800 sittings'.

In the days before the First World War the church flourished but between the Wars the congregation declined and there were suggestions that it should be closed. Happily this did not happen and when the Church of St. Andrew was destroyed during the 1941 blitz St. Catherine's, although damaged, was saved owing to the devotion of the Curate and members of the congregation acting as firewatchers. Perhaps the final years of its existence are the most glorious, as, damaged and scarred, it served as the acting Mother Church of Plymouth.

When the war was over and the reconstruction of St. Andrew's was complete, the congregation returned to the older church and St. Catherine's was handed over to the City for demolition in accordance with municipal re-planning. The site is now used as a car park for the Council House.

This church, outstanding in that it had been faced with Dartmoor granite and the product of that great architect John Foulston, is now gone and nothing remains but memories.

Some stalls for the clergy now at St. Michael's, West Hoe.

Note: Lectern to St. Philip, Weston Mill.

Church of St. Chad, Whitleigh.

In 1896 a Kelly College Mission was started in Moon St, Devonport. Five years later a permanent Church of St. Chad was built on a site given by Lord St. Leven. This served the Morice Town area for many years until the post war period, when the building came within the Dockyard extension. Renovated and modernised, it then became the Church of St. Lo and it now stands just inside the new Albert Gate of the Yard.

In 1952 services were started at Whitleigh, first in a tent, then in a school hall, and later in an old farmhouse, where accommodation for the priest was also provided.

A permanent church was obviously necessary and in 1955 the foundation stone was laid by the Bishop of Plymouth, the Rt. Rev. Norman H, Clarke. The architect was A.C. Luxton.
After completion, the new church was dedicated to St. Chad in 1956, and a new parish created.
The organ and altar furnishings came from the old church of St. Chad (now St. Lo). The High Altar came from the Church of St. James the Great at Keyham (closed 1951) which had been the original.
Mother Church of St. Chad. This is a fine modern red brick structure overlooking Whitleigh Green. The statue of St.Chad is mounted on the front of the building.

Charles Church.

To start the account of Charles, we can do no better than to quote from the plaque at present nearby: 'Prior to 1634 there was but one parish church in Plymouth, St. Andrew's, but in that year the town petitioned King Charles 1st for permission to divide the old Parish into two and to build a second church.
It was not until 1640, however, that letters patent permitting the church to be built received the Royal Assent.
Work was commenced immediately on a site somewhat to the west of the old Carmelite Friary, but building operations were suspended during the siege of Plymouth 1642-1646 and the church was not completed until 1658. The tower is dated 1657. The church was dedicated in 1665. The first spire, made of wood and covered with lead, was built in 1707-1708. This spire was taken down and the present stone spire erected in 1767.
The building was regarded as one of the finest post Reformation Gothic churches in the Kingdom. Various additions and alterations, such as the additions of the porches and vestry, and the removal of the galleries, were carried out in the 19th century.
Prior to the Second World War, the graveyard surrounding the church extended to over an acre, but in the construction of the new

Exeter Street, the human remains were removed and the graveyard no longer exists.

On the night of March 21st/22nd, 1941, the church was wholly gutted by fire as a result of a heavy air raid, and until 1957 the ruins remained in a derelict condition.

The Church Authorities having decided that the church was not to be rebuilt, the Plymouth Corporation purchased the site and in 1957, with the assistance of the Ministry of Works, carried out the preservation works.

The Church now forms a fitting memorial to the civilian population of Plymouth who lost their lives due to enemy air attacks on the City during the Second World War.'

The above certainly gives an excellent potted history, but other accounts suggest that in the reign of King Charles 1, the relations between the King and the town were somewhat strained - religion and politics being the stumbling blocks.

In 1634, Robert Trelawney, the mayor, petitioned the King to erect a new church. There had been quarrels with the King over St. Andrew's and it was thought that the erection of a new church might lessen the dissension. The King delayed but approval was finally given in 1641. Building began immediately, but as we have seen, was interrupted by the Siege, when the incomplete building was used for the stabling of the horses of the defenders. Church completed in 1657 but spire not added until 1708. Consecrated 1665. Known locally as 'the New Church!' it was described as being a mixture of 'Gothic and Classic.....the reredos is an arcade of nine arches supported on marble pillars with foliated capitals...' It had a three decker pulpit. Considerable alterations took place in 1735 and 1759 and it was restored in 1864. In 1888, unsightly doors and pews were replaced, north and south galleries taken down, vaults drained and north west porch erected. In 1882 the high walls surrounding the graveyard were taken down and iron railings put in their place. A pre War account describes the church as 'a stone building in the Gothic style, consisting of chancel, nave, aisles, south and west porches, and a lofty western tower with spire, containing ten bells cast in 1782, 1856 and 1898, six having previously been recast in 1709.' The account goes on to say that there were many monuments and there were 900 sittings. Owing to the expansion of the town, a chapel-of-ease became desirable. This was built and opened under the name of Charles Chapel consecrated 1829. Later, in 1874, this became the Parish Church of St. Luke.

Charles Church was destroyed by fire owing to enemy action in 1941, and it is sad to relate that amid so much heroism, the ten bells were stolen.

One was found later on the city dump. During the blitz all bells except two crashed to the ground.

In 1954 the Churches of Charles and St. Lukes became joined under the name of 'The Church of Charles with St. Luke' - a case of the Daughter church welcoming the Mother.

Later, St. Luke was closed (now used as additional premises for the Public Library) and the church combined with St. Matthias, which, in 1964 became known as 'The Church of Charles with St. Matthias' - its present name.

The Parish of Charles was very large and eight daughter churches have been formed from it:

1829 Charles Chapel, later St. Luke
1855 St. John the Evangelist
1870 Emmanuel
1876 St. Jude
1887 St. Matthias
1904 St. Augustine
1907 St. Simon
1910 St. Gabriel

Charles Church was never rebuilt but was partly restored in 1952. Although roofless, it has occasionally been used (Civil Defence services have been held there). It now stands isolated in the middle of a busy traffic roundabout, as a permanent memorial to Plymouth's war dead.

Some have advocated the complete demolition of Charles in the name of 'progress'. Happily, this suggestion has been resisted by the Civic Authorities and it remains as a fitting memorial to those of our townspeople who made the ultimate sacrifice. We have no future if we forget the past.

The Household of the Faith.

The Rev. R.S. Chalk was curate at Charles Church from 1932 to 1936 and was Priest in Charge at St. Philip's at Weston Mill 1952 - 1955 and Vicar until 1959.
To quote from a letter by Mr. Chalk to the Western Morning News in 1953, we have the following:
' ......Dr. Robert Hawker, Vicar of Charles from 1780 to 1787, was without doubt one of the greatest figures of Plymouth. His long ministry marked one of the most progressive periods in her history. As a scholar, preacher, pioneer-organiser, and, above all, champion of the poor, he was without an equal in the West in his day. Now his remains lie forgotten amid the desecrated rubble of the church he served and his memorial is soon to perish with him ....."
His first big step on being elected Vicar was to establish the first Church Sunday School in Plymouth, and presumably, apart from sporadic preliminary efforts, the second in the kingdom. Let Dr. Hawker's own words describe what took place. He wrote "The Household of the Faith in the Parish of Charles, Plymouth, arose from very slender beginnings. The commencement bears date the Lord's Day, January 21st, 1787.
A few children gathered from the streets were first invited into a room hired for that purpose in Friary Court. The school opened with a prayer and at the close of the prayer the scholars sat down to learning. When the church going bell gave notice of the time of public worship, the newly gathered company were led in regular order to the House of God. And thus began the Sunday School in the Parish of Charles." Four years later, a School of Industry was added, and the whole moved to more commodious quarters in

Woolster St. Numbers were then 341. Dr. Hawker continues "But it was not until the year 1798 that the Sunday School and the School of Industry found a permanent dwelling place in a house of their own ....."'. The report then goes on to note the foundation being laid on 7th March and a modest mansion near the New Church (Charles) erected. The new school was called the Household of the Faith. Over the door of the building was the figure of a Sunday School Scholar.

Although Charles itself was destroyed in the blitz, the Household of the Faith in nearby Vennel St (adjoining the graveyard of the Plymouth Friends), survived.

About 1954, when the Charles roundabout was being constructed, the School which had lasted so long was demolished. Happily, the statue representing the scholar survives and is now in the Church Hall of St. Matthias. Mr. Chalk mentioned that there was a local tradition that she turned a page of her bible every night and remarks that if this is so, she must have now come to the last page of Revelation - the demolition being imminent.

So ended Plymouth's first Sunday School, the Household of the Faith. It is good to know, however, that the institution is kept alive at the Church of Charles with St. Matthias on North Hill. (q.v.)

Christ Church, Eton Place.

Built in 1845 to the design of George Wightwick (an associate of Foulston). The silver trowel was also employed at similar ceremonies at Holy Trinity, Emmanuel and St. Jude's. Church was consecrated in 1886. A Parish had been formed in 1847 from that of St. Andrew, to which it was later returned.

An old report notes the church as being '...of stone in the Perpendicular style. Consisting of a clerestoried nave, aisles, west porch and belfry containing one bell. Church restored and screen added in 1896. 880 sittings'.

William Derry, donor of the well-known clock and Mayor in 1862 and 1879, was a worshipper here.

A notable event was when the building was struck by lightning in 1913: the roof was damaged, one of the pinnacles fell down and the belfry door was blown into the chancel. The remaining pinnacle was taken down and a 12ft. cross erected on the gable.

The church was in a somewhat out of the way place until the cutting through of Western Approach when it appeared on a main thoroughfare. However, when the North Cross roundabout was being constructed in 1966, the building was demolished, the site now being a grassy open space overlooking the City Centre.

Happily, not all of Christ Church has been lost, as the organ and carved screen have been installed in the war damaged and now rebuilt Church of St. Augustine, Lipson Vale.

Some pews now at St. Michael, West Hoe.

The Church of St. Edward the Martyr, Eggbuckland.

The name Egg Buckland or Eggbuckland appears to come from that of a Saxon Lord who held this land by charter. His name was Heche, hence Heche's Boke Londe or Heche's book land, which in due course was contracted to its present Eggbuckland.

Almost certainly a church existed here in Saxon times and it is known that in 1248 it was in the gift of the Priory of Plympton. The church we know at present was built about 1430, the tower, nave, south aisle, porch and one bell are all part of the original (1430) building, although enlargement and repair began in 1864. Additional bells were installed in 1682 and 1768 and it was not until 1882 that all the bells were taken down and recast into the present peal of six bells. The legend on the old bell ran: 'With my living voice, I drive away all harmful things'.

The 1864 enlargement mentioned consisted in general of adding the north aisle and the chancel and then little change took place until the 1930's when some restoration was carried out, notably the installation of new oaken pews and the completion of the barrel roof and screen. Further restoration was done in 1959.

With the increase in population and the expansion of the town, St. Edward the Martyr became the Mother church of those erected at Laira (St. Mary the Virgin) and at Glenholt.

This is a most picturesque old church with a square tower surmounted by four pinnacles and containing a clock, has some fine stained glass and a beautiful rood screen. The carved stone font, too, is of some note. Many memorials on the walls make interesting reading. A splendid church which is well worth a visit.

Parish Church of Emmanuel.

In the mid-twenties of the 19th century, the 'gentry', wanting to escape from the growing congestion of Plymouth, began to build outside the town.

Large houses were constructed round Compton village, Foulston himself building a 'thatched cottage' in the fields at Townshend Hill. By 1831 the population had increased to 229.

There was no place of worship in the vicinity the nearest being Charles Church about two miles away. The need was recognised and a Capt. Bremer who had built himself a large house known as the 'Priory', gave a site for the erection of a small chapel. When this was complete it was licensed in 1836 and served by the Rev. G. Hall-Parlby (see notes on St. Pancras) for 17 years. By 1840 the district began to have an institutional life of its own, with its church, school, inn, gentry, yeomen and labourers.

The chapel was enlarged in 1858 to seat 200 people but by 1860 the need for a larger church was becoming obvious. The district was still growing, Hartley reservoir had been constructed, and houses erected at Thornhill. Buildings were also projected for Collings Park and Hartley (Hartley Villas).

In 1866, the vicar of Charles Church and the curate in charge of Compton initiated action to have a new church built at Mannamead.

On his death bed, a Mr. Revel, the owner of land in the district, asked his wife and daughter to give a site for the new church, provided it was called 'Emmanuel', as he had been educated at Emmanuel College, Cambridge. The site, then, was offered free by Mrs. Betsy and Miss Elisabeth Revel.

Mr. Reid, an architect, offered his services without charge and a sum of £565 was offered by those attending the original meeting in connection with this project.

After some delay, the corner stone was laid by Mr. Greaves, vicar of Charles. In June, 1869 building went ahead and was complete by 1870. A point of note here is that the erection of Emmanuel coincided with the construction of the Guildhall, and excavated stone from the Guildhall site was used for the foundations of Emmanuel. A complication arose in that when the ground for the church had been given, the space in front had not been included, as this had been let to a Mr. Marshall who started to build villas thereon. After some work had been done it was realised that these houses would spoil the appearance of the church - being right in front of it - and it is assumed that the proximity was not desirable for other reasons. Arrangements were made to have the land conveyed to the Ecclesiastical Commissioner and when this had been done, the part completed houses were demolished, leaving a fine open space in the foreground of the church - a space that was probably very little encroached upon until the building of a bus-bay in 1975 or 1976.

Although the basic church had been completed in 1870 and the organ installed in 1876, certain additions were made later.

1880-1881   Nave completed, transepts, vestry and chancel added.

1895   Foundation stone of the tower was laid by the Mayor, Mr. F.W. Law. This was intended to have a spire, in fact, the early drawings show it but due to financial difficulties it was never constructed.

1904   Eight bells, weighing over four tons were dedicated.

1970   Centenary celebrations (church constructed 18th Sept.1870) were held.
             Commemorative tree planted by Mrs. E.L. Winnicott.

A daughter church, that of St. Paul at Efford, was built at Efford in 1964. At present this has no resident priest but is served from Emmanuel.

Emmanuel must have seen many changes; the regular passing of Baskerville's horse bus on the way to Roborough, the coming and going of the electric trams, road widening, and a constant stream of traffic which was unthought of in the days past. It remains, however, as a tribute to those men and women of goodwill whose faith enabled it to come into being.

Church of St. Francis, Honicknowle.

Situated in Little Dock Lane, this is a modern brick and concrete building of functional design. The foundation stone was laid by the Bishop of Exeter in 1939 and the church dedicated in September of the same year.

In 1956 a parish was created from that of St. Budeaux and the church consecrated.

Although a modern building, it does contain some interesting items. The old granite font came from Revelstoke and the organ from a private house at Mary Tavy. The tryptich over the Lady Altar is from the Church of St. Peter in Wyndham Square.

Perhaps the most striking feature is the mural behind the High Altar. Painted by the late Lewis Duckett, it represents St. Francis and the animals - a most attractive scene. Another interesting association with St. Peter's, as this has also a fine statue of St. Francis.

Externally a rather plain building with a small belfry containing one bell, yet the immediate impression on entering the church is one of brightness and cheerfulness.

The Parish Church of St. Gabriel.

At the turn of the century, the spread of the town necessitated a place of worship in the Hyde Park area, and for some time services were held in the gymnasium of Plymouth College. This was only a temporary measure and subsequently, the Rev. Trelawney Ross of Ham gave part of a field as a site for the proposed new church. Contributions to this end were made by the Free Masons of Devon. The foundation stone was laid in 1910 with Masonic ceremony and the building was started, consisting originally of what is now the western end - four bays and the nave. Not until 1924 was the eastern half of the nave and the chancel added.

About the same time, a corrugated iron hut (obtained from Hyde Park School) was erected to serve as a Church Hall. It was intended to replace this hut by a more permanent structure, but this has never been done and it still exists to serve its original purpose.

During the last war the crypt was used as a rest centre.

The Lady Chapel was built in 1955 and about the same time the bell turret was added, Later, a vicarage was erected on a plot of ground adjoining the church.

The church is a dignified structure but perhaps one of its unusual features is the war memorial just inside the church, near the entrance. It commemorates our own service and civilian dead. Noted also are the names of four young German flyers whose plane was shot down over the City. The names are: Ernst Krefeld, Hans Scheide, Adolf Schmidt and Wilhelm Feuchter. They were buried in Ford Park Cemetery by the present vicar, Mr. C.G.H Treneer. The inclusion of their names with those of our people seems to be a charitable gesture.

Another feature of note is the Chapel of St. Christopher at the west end of the church. This was given by the Scout Troop and the old Scouts.

As with many churches, St. Gabriel's has seen many changes. When it was built in 1910 it was in a growing area, and although electric trams ran in front of it at that time, fields existed on the western side. Now the trams have gone and the church is surrounded by houses, but the church still stands to fulfil its original purpose.

The Church of St. George, East Stonehouse.

In the days when most houses were made of wood, it is thought that in this district was one of stone, hence the name. The district is known as East Stonehouse to differentiate from the 'West Stonehouse' believed to be on the other side of the Hamoaze. We do find West Stonehouse mentioned in 1602.

At the end of the 15th century there were two chapels: St. George's, which existed on a site opposite the end of Emma Place, and that of St. Lawrence at Devil's Point. We know that the chapel of St. Lawrence was in being in 1472 and that it was removed in the 18th century to make way for the construction of the Royal William Victualling Yard.

The chapel of St. George stood in a yard surrounded by trees "...wherein were stiles which had to be mended to keep the hogs out..."

About 1787 the old chapel was demolished and the Church of St. George erected in its place. It survived until 1941 when it was wrecked by enemy action. The damage was somewhat freakish, as apart from destroying the body of the church, the tower was split down the middle, leaving only one half standing. This remained until the early 1950's when it was demolished and now, as far as is known, no trace remains.

Deprived of their church, the congregation combined with those of St. Paul at the other end of Durnford St., that church then becoming 'The Parish Church of St. George and St. Paul'.

Pre-war photos show St. George to have been a fine large church; now all that is known to remain is the brass cross from the altar which is preserved at the Church of St. Paul.

As a postscript, it is said that the stone of the old St. Lawrence's Chapel at Devils Point was used to build the fake chapel or 'folly' on the Mount Edgcumbe Estate. This seems reasonable as it was only necessary to remove the stone across a narrow stretch of water.

Parish of Southway, Church of the Holy Spirit.

In the entrance hall of the church is a table noting 'Southway Community Church, 4th June, 1960'. Originally a daughter church of Tamerton, it became a parish in 1961.

The building, in the centre of a new estate, is modern in concept consisting of a hall and church combined, with a curtained off portion at one end containing the altar, organ, lectern and some seating. The major part of the building is the hall with a stage at the opposite end to the altar. Consequently by removing the division, extra seating can be provided for church services as occasion demands. For other needs, the hall can be used with the small chapel curtained off.

The organ, made by 'Fred Tucker of Plymouth', is old but excellent. Quite obviously it came from an older church - perhaps one blitzed during the last war. The lectern, too, probably has a similar history. The metal part of the font is thought to have come from a ship. There are other interesting items in the building of which the origins are not known.

The building is of concrete construction with red brick cladding. It has a small spire. The Vicarage is adjacent. A small but attractive church which fits in well with its surroundings.

Church of Holy Trinity, Southside Street.

This was built in 1840 by the Rev. John Hatchard as a chapel-of-ease to St. Andrew's. It seated more than 1,000 persons and was located at the back of what is now the gin distillery.

An early account describes it as '....in Southside St. and Friar's Lane. Built in 1842 in the Doric order. Consists of nave, chancel, galleries aisles, with a north porch and a tower on west side'. Later, in 1842, it became a Parish in its own right, and, no doubt due to the needs of the district, became the Mother Church of St. Saviour (see separate notes). Parson Barnes was the vicar at this time.

Holy Trinity was badly damaged during the blitz and has been almost totally demolished. Remains as exist can be seen at the back of a car park of a firm supplying goods for freezers.

These remains are just the east wall - or part of it - in which traces of the windows are still visible.

Looking across from the Wall to Friar's Lane can be discerned the old Vicarage, now used for other purposes.

It seems in the past that this district was very unsavoury and that the Rev. Hatchard and Rev. Barnes (both of St. Andrew's), together with the Unitarian Minister, the Rev. Odgers, had much to do with the welfare of the area. It is certain that they were men of good will and no little degree of courage.

Parish Church of St. James the Less, Millbay.

This parish was created from that of St. Andrews in 1847. A site was secured (that now occupied by a school at the rear of the Duke of Cornwall Hotel) and work started in 1858 to the design of Mr. Piers St. Aubyn. This must have been a developing area as the railway had only just reached the district and Millbay Station built a few years before (1849).

Foundation stones for the church were laid, work being partly carried out by Russian P.O.Ws from the nearby Millbay Barracks. By 1861 much work had been done and the building consecrated. About 1864 the nave was started and schools built. A house was also obtained for use as the vicarage. The church held 600 persons. In 1870 the parish was extended 'to take in under the Hoe and Millbay docks'. The church was now virtually complete and although it is assumed that the original plans provided for a tower and spire, these never materialised.

In 1884 a fine carved oak roof, both gilded and painted, was added, together with an iron grill and tessellated floor. The Vicar and Guild of St. Charles the Martyr gave a beautiful chancel screen and gates, and they also provided two alabaster pulpits and a decorative canopy over the high altar. The ornamentation of the church was said to be outstanding.

From the first, St. James the Less had been associated with the full teaching of the Catholic Faith and it was in the year 1884 that incense was used for the first time.

During the summer months, owing to its location the church attracted many holidaymakers and many naval personnel attended at all times.

The building was almost completely destroyed in the 1941 blitz and was never rebuilt. This marks the passing of an outstanding church, a sailor once remarked to the vicar "….. if there were more churches like this, Sir, we should not forget God".

The dedication of St. James the Less has now passed to a fine new church at Ham.

Postscript: In 1941 when the church had been hit by incendiaries, a resident in the area stated that she watched it burn. Owing to bombing the water supply had failed and nothing could be done to save it. On the same evening the stables of Mr. Stoneman nearby were ablaze and the terrified horses were released and saved by those people in the neighbourhood - an act of bravery which passed without special mention in the days when the country was united against a common enemy.

Some of the stonework was used to rebuild St. Michael's at Stoke.

Church of St. James the Less, Ham.

Plans were approved in 1955 for the building of a new church and vicarage at Ham. The first turf was cut in 1957 by the Rev. G. Sunderland. Also present at the ceremony was the Rev. T.D. Davis who at that time was vicar of St. Mark's, Ford.

Foundation stone laid by the Bishop of Plymouth, Dr. Norman H. Clarke, and when finished the church was dedicated by the Bishop of Exeter, Dr. R.C. Mortimer.

Perhaps we cannot do better than quote from the notice inside the church itself: '…… This church derives its dedication from St.

James the Less, West Hoe, Plymouth (1861-1941). It replaces the temporary church of St. Anne, Swilly, which was built as a daughter church of St. Mark, Ford. The bell and pews were formerly in the church of St. James the Great, Devonport, and the high altar and choir stalls in the church of Our Lady and St. Mary Magdelene, Cattedown. The east window was designed by Sir Ninian Cooper'.

St. James the Less also has associations with the church of St. Stephen in George Street, Devonport. The altar of St. Stephen at the rear of the church bears this notice: 'This chapel has been furnished as a memorial to St. Stephen's church, Devonport (1858-1941) destroyed by enemy action. The war damage payment for the ruin of the building provided most of the money to erect this church.

The statue of St. Stephen is a replica of the one which formed part of the screen in the old church. Together with the altar cross, it was carved from wood of the figure on the crucifix erected outside the church in memory of the fallen of the parish (1914-1918) which was later removed and almost destroyed by enemy action. The furnishings of the chapel are a gift of former members of the congregation of St. Stephen's, Devonport'.

The crucifix referred to in the previous quotation had quite a history. Erected after the first World War by the vicar, Rev. H.H. Leeper, as a memorial to the fallen. There was some local opposition to the form the memorial had taken, and it was subsequently taken down and put into store with a firm in Cattedown who had been responsible for its carving and construction. During the 1939-1945 war the factory was bombed and the damaged crucifix was later found floating in The Sound. It was rescued and, as we have seen, carvings made from it now form part of the altar of St. Stephen, a happy ending for Father Leeper's efforts.

To return to the church as it is now. Structurally it has a steel frame and is faced with red brick on the outside. Designed by Messrs. Evans and Sloggett, it presents a pleasant sight when viewed from

Ham Drive. It lies back from the road and the surrounding trees give it a most attractive appearance.

A light, spacious and cheerful church having many interesting features, an outstanding one of which is the fine window behind the altar - a beautiful piece of modern stained glass which is well worth seeing.

In 1977, the organ from Keyham Methodist Church, built by Mr. T. Heleid, is now being fitted at St. James the Less.

Church of St. James the Great, Devonport.

Owing to the expansion of the Dockyard and the building of houses in the Keyham area, a church in the district became desirable.

The original site was secured by Capt. Sellon. R.N. (it is assumed that he was a relation of the Miss Sellon, who together with the Rev. George Rundle Prynne of St. Peter's did so much good work during the cholera epidemic of 1849). The foundation stone was laid by Admiral Gage 1849 and the church built at a cost of £6,000 of which £4,000 was contributed by the Admiralty in consideration of a sufficient number of sittings being set apart for the use of Government employees. The church was consecrated in 1851, schools opened in 1863 and Vicarage added in 1868.

St. James the Great was situated at the junction of St. James Place (now St Leo Place) and Keyham Road.

It was a fine limestone building but owing to changes in the district, notably the post war Dockyard extension, it was demolished in 1958 and the present flats built on the site.

No trace of the former church now remains except a few parts of the limestone boundary walls, although it is good to know that the high altar is now at the church of St. Chad at Whitleigh and the bell and pews went to St. James the Less at Ham.

St. James the Great is no more but it will be remembered as having served the district well for over 100 years.

Church of St. John the Baptist, Duke Street, Devonport.

This was built by subscription in 1799 at a cost of £8,000. Situated at the top of Duke Street partly opposite the Unitarian Christ Church, it was a very plain building externally with a rather unusual pillared tower over the main entrance.
The 'History of Devonport' notes that '…..but for its queer cupola it might be mistaken for a tithe barn'. The main door was on the lower side and approached by flights of stone steps.
Internally it had three aisles and an elliptical gallery. It is noted as neat in appearance and had a good organ.
This part of Devonport has seen much change and the church of St. John, which once was amid a busy part of the town, has now gone and the flats built on the site now overlook the post war Dockyard extension. One of the few remaining landmarks in the immediate vicinity is the Devonport Public Library and Museum, now used in the main as a Motor Taxation Office.
Organ now at the church of St. Michael, Stoke.

The Church of St. John the Evangelist, Sutton on Plym.

In 1844 Charles Church was becoming overcrowded and Queen Victoria declared part of the Parish of Charles to be the District of Sutton on Plym. Land known as Friar's Piece was obtained and by the terms of the deed, the land when consecrated was to be used for ecclesiastical purposes for ever.
The new church was designed by Benjamin Ferry, who had studied under Pugin, the famous R.C. architect. The new church was not consecrated until 1855 when it became known as St John the Evangelist. Originally it consisted of chancel, nave, aisles, north chapel, northwest porch, and a tower with a spire containing one bell, which had been cast at Whitechapel and weighed over 300cwt. The organ was installed in 1859 and ten years later the pulpit and reredos were added.

The rood screen was given in 1872 and the Lady Chapel built in 1883. The oaken rood which came from Oberammergau dates from 1912, in which year the font was moved to its present position. The font is of some note as it is carved out of a solid block of marble. Altar and reredos in the south aisle were given in 1915, and at the end of the first World War a stone calvary was erected outside the church on the north side as a memorial to the fallen.

St John the Evangelist was badly damaged during the blitz of 1941 and the 1883 Lady Chapel completely wrecked. Rebuilt in 1954, it is outstanding with its carved front of the altar depicting the symbols of the Mother of God, the lily and the crown. The carving was by Miss Pinwell who is well known for her work in Plymouth churches. Some years before, Miss Pinwell had carved the beautiful font cover.

The windows are of some note. In particular the new east window shows St Matthew, St Mark, St Luke and St John, symbolised respectively by an angel, lion, ox and eagle. The 1859 organ had been rebuilt in 1937.

In 1971, owing to shortage of clergy and the falling numbers of those attending, it was decided that the church should be closed. A booklet was produced to mark the end of this historic building and the termination of so many years of service to the community. Happily, due to energetic efforts the closure did not occur, the number of worshippers has increased and St John's continues to be a power for good in the area.

The church of St Mary Magdalen in nearby Alvington Street was a daughter church and later became a separate parish (see under separate note).

Parish Church of St Jude.

During the latter half of the 19th century more places of worship became necessary as the town expanded. This was the case at St Jude's and at first services were held in a room over a baker's shop in Salem Street. Money became available through the generosity of some prominent citizens to enable land at what was then known as Higher Barn Park to be secured as the site for the new church. The foundation stone was laid in 1875 by Bishop Temple, the silver trowel employed at the ceremony was also the one used on similar occasions at Holy Trinity, Christ Church and Emmanuel. The completed building was consecrated in 1876, as a daughter church to Charles and the first Vicar was the Rev. T.H. Howard who had previously been a Curate at the mother church.

Practical difficulties soon arose as during a fierce storm in 1877, the lack of proper ducts for the rainwater resulted in damage to the roof and to some windows. Lack of money too prevented the completion of the heating apparatus necessitating the temporary installation of gas heaters. This seems to have been satisfactory until the heating as designed was finished and working.

As no proper organ was available a hired harmonium was used for a time but through the financial assistance of Rev. T.A. Bewes a proper organ was obtained in 1878. The first few years must have seen many changes as it was in 1878 that the London and S.W. Railway brought the lines through the adjacent Pomeroy's Field to terminate its main line at what became Friary Station (on the site of a 12th century Carmelite Friary). With the digging of the cutting and the erection of the station, the district must have been one of considerable activity.

In 1882 the tower and spire were erected, again through the generosity of Rev. T.A. Bewes, who in 1887 also helped towards the cost of a church room.

The church is said to be in the early English style and hold 630 persons. The architect was James Hine. The ornamentation of the capitals of the pillars is very attractive and full of detail, well worth close inspection. At the back of the altar the reredos relates to the Creed and the Ten Commandments. Another feature is that at the back of the church is a cork model of the building made from the plans of the architects (Messrs Hines & Odgers) by the Rev. John

Saunders. This model was constructed by Mr. Saunders when he was in his 80's and took him a year to complete.

As has been noted, the church has seen many changes. Once it was in fairly rural surroundings - now it stands at busy crossroads in circumstances its builders could never have envisaged. But although so many things have changed, the work of the church continues unaltered in 1977 as it did in 1877.

Chapel of St Katherine, Citadel.

The present chapel stands upon the site of the former Chapel of St Katherine, licenced for services by Bishop Brantyingham in 1371 for use of the people in the Sutton Pool area and was a chapel-of-ease to St Andrew. An old audit book shows that it was involved with the Plymouth garrison even then, an extract being:- 'Itm pd to ye hermyte of seynt Katyn to mend ye tile in ye Chapell ye whch was broken wit ye gvnne . . . iii j d.' which suggests that 'ye hermyte' may have been a bit of a d.i.y. builder.

Worship continued at the chapel but it was demolished in 1666 when the Citadel was built. A new chapel was constructed and completed in 1668 with a nave 59 feet long by 25 feet wide, and with walls nearly 3 feet thick.

Considerable alterations were made in 1845 when the north and south transepts were added and a west end extension made to the nave. General the Hon. Sir Henry Murray, who was the Governor of the Citadel at that time, presented the existing fine stone font. It was at this time, too, that three galleries were added in the transepts, but due to lack of space (or poor planning) there is no way to these galleries from within the chapel itself, the only way of entrance being from the outside of the building - a somewhat unusual feature.

The public may join the services held here and the chapel is well worth a visit. Of note are the frescoes in the chancel. They were painted by an NCO who was stationed there in the 1914/18 war, a

member of the Royal Engineers, he later went to France and was killed. Regrettably, his name is not known but his excellent paintings still remain. The chapel has a two manual organ built in 1928 and a fine set of communion vessels made in 1762.
An interesting and historic building which deserves to be better known. It now seats 475 persons.

Church of St. Lo, Devonport Dockyard.

This building was previously the Church of St. Chad in Moon Street, Morice Town. After the war the Dockyard boundaries were extended and certain streets were taken in, including the Church of St. Chad.
The building was taken over by the Yard and renamed St. Lo. It was renovated and modernised and a fine hall added.
The original Dockyard Church of St. Lo was the third oldest ecclesiastical building in Devonport being built in 1700. It appears to have been paid for initially by officers and men of H.M. ships and through the initiative of George St. Leo, Commissioner of the Yard at that time.
The building was demolished in 1817 and another erected, additions being made to this second church in 1820. It survived until 1941 when it was destroyed during the blitz.
As we have seen, when the Church of St Chad was absorbed by the Yard, it assumed the name of St. Lo. (see also notes on St. Chad). The organ and altar furnishings went to the new Church of St. Chad at Whitleigh.

Church of St. Luke, Richmond Walk, Devonport.

This was not a very well-known church, possibly owing to its rather out of the way location. It exists alongside the works of Messrs. Crockerell Builders, on a site which is now an Admiralty car park about 100 yards west of Webber's Slip.

A Miss Collins provided the funds to build this small church about 1911. Destroyed in the blitz of March 1941, nothing now remains except a small brass cross which stood on the altar. Happily, this cross is now preserved at the Parish Church of Stoke Damerel (q.v).

Richmond Walk, once a busy spot with a rail terminal (Ocean Quay) is now becoming a very active place again, with its boating marina and the new luxury flats built on the location where passengers from trans-atlantic liners once landed.

Church of St. Luke, Plymouth.

It was decided in 1827 to build a chapel-of-ease to Charles. Foundation stone was laid in 1828 and the building known as Charles Chapel was completed and consecrated in 1829. Situated in Tavistock Place, at the rear of what is now the Public Library, it is said to have seated 1,700 and an early description is '…. a building of stone of the Doric order …. consists of chancel, nave, aisles, west porch and turret containing one bell. At the east end is a memorial window and there are thirteen other stained windows….'
A parish was created in 1874 and the chapel then became known as The Parish Church of St. Luke.

A picture, obviously taken in the last century, shows a plain but dignified building with a square centrally placed tower, just above roof level, the top being supported on twelve pillars and the whole surmounted by a weather vane. In front of the church are trees. A later picture shows the top of the tower has been removed.

Internally the build was very spacious with galleries on three sides and a fine organ at the rear. Another photo shows that it had two pulpits, both of wood, and a wooden lectern. The reredos in stone appears to consist of biblical passages; the arch over the chancel was inscribed: 'Christ Jesus came into the world to save sinners' and in front and above the altar 'THE RESURRECTION' in large letters.

Another inscription of note is that on the gallery in front of the organ, which reads: 'O sing unto the Lord a new song'. It is not known how many of these early features remain.

During the blitz of March 1941, Charles Church was destroyed and in 1954 the churches of Charles and St. Luke were joined, St Luke then becoming the Parish Church of the united parish.

At a Thanksgiving service in December 1954, the Bishop of Plymouth spoke of the Daughter welcoming the Mother home. For a short while after the destruction of Charles the congregation had worshipped at St Matthias but later returned to St. Luke.

In 1961, owing to planning requirements, it was decided to demolish St. Luke's but this did not, in fact, happen. The Parish Church of Charles with St. Luke again joined St. Matthias and in 1964 that church became officially known as the Parish Church of Charles with St. Matthias.

The old church of St. Luke still stands and is at present used as an annexe to the City Library. (A false ceiling has been installed. Many stained glass windows remain).

An unusual feature, and one that still remains, is the outside pulpit which faces the rear of the Library. An inscribed tablet on it reads: 'In the hope that it may further God's work and in loving memory of Caroline Louisa, wife of Frederick Courtney, fifth bishop of Nova Scotia and from 1865 to 1870 incumbent of Charles Chapel (now St. Luke's Church), this pulpit is erected 1913'.

There has been much demolition in the area and the future fate of St. Luke's is not known. Although changes must occur in the name of progress, it seems a pity if such an historic building should be swept away. (See also notes on Charles and on St Matthias).

Church of St. Mark, Ford.

The foundation stone for this church was laid in 1874 by the Bishop of Exeter. The chancel was built in 1876 and the church completed by the addition of nave and aisles in 1892. The building is said to be in the Early English Style.

Perhaps the most interesting item in connection with St. Mark's is its association with Robert Falcon Scott (Scott of the Antarctic). He was a choirboy here and a very nice picture of him as a young man is found in the vestry. A large wooden carving of Scott dressed in arctic clothes exists behind the choir stalls. Scott himself, lived at Outlands on the site of what is now St. Bartholomew Church, Milehouse.
St Mark's was the mother church of St. Anne's at Swilly, a temporary wooden structure which served the district until the erection of St. James the Less at Ham.
At the time of building the church of St. Mark it must have overlooked a swampy valley and stream. Now after much infilling, this has become St. Levan Road, from parts of which in very bad weather, some flooding still occurs.

Church of St. Martin, Peverell.

A site (now the Junction of Tavistock Road and Weston Park Road) was given by the Bayly brothers of Tor for the building of a new church at Peverell, This was to be named St. Martin's.
The crypt was constructed and used for divine service but due to lack of money the church properly was never finished.
In 1939 when St. Pancras was damaged, services were transferred to St. Martin's Crypt until the repair of the former church in 1956. Services were then discontinued at the Crypt and it was later demolished. The walls of the crypt of St. Martin could still be seen for some time afterwards but these have now gone.
All that is visible at present is a small piece of the limestone wall on the west side, the ground having been cleared. It appears that the City intends it to remain an open grassy space.

Church of St. Mary Magdelene, Alvington St, Cattedown.

Believed to be more correctly called 'The Church of St. Mary the Virgin and St. Mary Magdelene' this was the church of the parish

created from that of St. John the Evangelist in 1911.
Described as consisting of a chancel, nave, north and south aisles and a bell turret containing one bell. Built of limestone, it had 500 sittings. The building can still be seen but is no longer used as a church.
After closure, the High Altar and choir stalls were incorporated in the new church of St. James the Less at Ham.
Now used as a store by the South Western Electricity Board, traces of the original church still remain such as ceiling decoration and even one small stained glass window. Externally, it still looks very much as it did formerly although certain carvings over the main entrance appear to have been covered over perhaps with the idea of preserving them.
See also notes on St. James the Less and on St. John the Evangelist.

Church of St. Mary, James Street, Devonport.

Situated in the middle of James St. and adjoining the Dockyard wall, this church was erected about 1850 to the design of Sir. J. Piers St. Aubyn. Said to be in the Decorated style, the chancel being paved with Minton tiles. Some fine stained glass is also noted.
Recorded as having been 'in the patronage of the Crown and the Bishop of Exeter alternatively', it cost £6000, this money being partly raised by public subscription.
Personal memories are that it had commodious rooms under the church proper and that it was the home of the '7th Devonport Scouts' (this about 1914). The building was destroyed in the blitz of 1941 when so many of our local buildings were lost. The site is now occupied by a block of flats and just to the northern side are the high rise flats known as Tavy House.
St. Mary's lives on in the memories of many older natives of Devonport, if not so much for the church itself as for one of the past Vicars the Rev. G.A. Bennett. He is remembered as a white-

haired, saintly man, who always had a kindly word or a smile for all, particularly the children.

Organ now at St. Bartholomew's.

Parish Church of St. Mary, Tamerton.

It is known that a church existed here in 1283 as the list of Vicars dates from about that time. In 1318 the dedication was to St. Mary. The church was rebuilt between 1400 and 1500 and the 78 feet high tower added. In 1775 new seating was installed and, regrettably, in 1794 a serious fire destroyed the parish registers thereby depriving us of much reference to the early history.

The churchyard was enlarged in 1870 and the gallery replaced by a tower screen in 1888.

Severe damage occurred in 1891, the year of the Great Blizzard, a blizzard of such severity that many accounts were written at the time and forms part of the history of the South West. At this time the north aisle was damaged but rebuilt in 1894, the choir stalls and organ being added at the same time.

A noticeable feature as one enters the building is the stocks in the porch. They were placed here in 1775 but details of their use does not survive. The choir vestry beneath the tower is probably on the original level but the church itself, judging from the fact that the bases of the pillars have been covered, appears to have had the floor raised by about two feet. The tower clock dates from 1897 and if one looks around the churchyard the earliest gravestone to be found is of 1723.

It is not possible in a short account to describe the church completely. Set in beautiful surroundings it contains much of interest. The roof bosses are said to be outstanding and the 16th century pulpit is of some note. Many memorials exist, in particular the Gorges Memorial.

The church possesses some fine plate (now kept at Buckland Abbey).

The patron of the living is H.M. the Queen which explains the Royal Coat of Arms over the porch door. Because of this patronage, the choir is entitled to wear red cassocks.

A fine church hall has been added in 1974 for use by the whole community.

In these short notes so many points of interest have been missed. A visit to this church which has served for so many years is a 'must'.

St. Mary the Virgin, Laira.

A small school and chapel were built at Crabtree and licenced by Bishop Temple in 1874. Its use was partly to serve the military garrison at Efford Fort which accounts for the sites being given by the War Department. This chapel was originally served from Eggbuckland although in later years there was a resident priest, the Rev. J.T. Merchant.

A site for a new church was given by Mrs. L. Clarke of Efford Manor. The foundation stone was laid in 1911, the church being complete and consecrated in 1914 by Bishop Robertson. The consecration ceremony was marked by a disturbance, apparently caused by members of the Kensit party, who were very much against any high church practices and were noted for their aggressive tactics. A Kensit preacher attempted to address the Bishop, and this, together with the beating of tin cans and jeering caused some unpleasantness. The police were asked to intervene to prevent the recurrence of such disorderly and intolerant behaviour. The parish was formed in 1931, a parish hall erected in 1932 and a vicarage in 1962.

The church is unfinished in appearance as although it is obvious that the original design provided for a much larger church, the nave and tower were never completed. Even so the building has many attractive features; the altars have wooden backgrounds, there is a fine wooden pulpit and the carved stone font with its wooden cover is of some note.

The church celebrated its Jubilee in 1964 and owing to the considerable growth in the area, the scope and responsibility of St. Mary the Virgin has increased greatly.

A fine church which it is hoped will some day be completed.

Church of St. Matthew, Stonehouse.

As early as 1873 a Mission Hall existed in Battery Street. Then a site in what is now Clarence Place was given by the Earl of Mount Edgcumbe and a competition held to choose the best design for the new church. That of Mr. H.J. Snell was selected and the church erected in 1875.

Schools and Mission Room were added in 1885. The Parish was created and subsequently returned to that of St. Peter in Wyndham Square.

Church was demolished about 1973 to make way for flats which have now been built on the site.

This area has seen many changes, once being a densely populated district. The old workhouse close to the church as well as many of the older dwellings in Stonehouse have been swept away and this part of the City is perhaps now more industrial than residential.

Older people will well remember the thriving and busy community that formerly existed.

Organ to St. Barnabas, Wilton Street.

Some pews to St. Boniface, St. Budeaux.

Lady Altar Cross to St. Peter, Wydham Square.

Church of St. Matthias.

Now correctly known as 'The parish church of Charles with St. Matthias' it occupies a commanding position on North Hill and with its 120 feet high tower is a landmark for miles around - even out at sea.

The church was erected on the grounds off North Hill House, the construction of the building being financed by Mrs. Anne Watts, who in 1885 formed a trust fund in memory of her husband for this purpose. Named the Church of St. Matthias it was complete and consecrated by the Bishop of Exeter in 1887. The cost of the building was £8000 and the architects were Messrs. Hine and Odgers. It became a parish church in 1889.

It is described as being '.... built in limestone in the Perpendicular style, consists of chancel, nave, aisles, west porch, and massive embattled tower 120 feet high. Reredos presented in 1891 by an anonymous donor. Church hall added in 1913....'

The reredos mentioned above was designed by Mr. G. Fellowes Prynne, the son of the Rev. George Rundle Prynne of St. Peters, Wyndham Square. Of note too are the stone carvings of St. Peter, St. Andrew, St. Paul and St. Matthias and beside the organ is a small carving of Cecilia, the patron saint of music. Oak panelling of the choir and sanctuary forms a war memorial to those who fell in the two recent wars.

During the last war the church was used by the congregations of Charles and of St. Augustine during some of the period after these buildings had been destroyed in the blitz. In 1962 the members of St. Luke, Charles and St. Matthias became joined, hence the present name of 'Charles with St. Matthias'.

Relics and documents of the old Charles Church and those of St. Luke are preserved within the church or are otherwise in safe keeping. The side chapel is dedicated to St. Luke and on the altar stands a gilded wooden cross from that church bearing the inscription: 'The wood in this cross was taken from the parish church of Charles, destroyed by enemy action 21st March 1941'. It had stood for nearly twenty years on the Holy Table at St. Luke's church. The Royal Coat of Arms, which formerly had occupied the central panel of the gallery at St. Luke's, is now placed over the vestry door of the north aisle.

Despite so many changes and so much destruction, the people of Charles, St. Luke and St. Matthias go forward together.

St. Matthias Mission Church.

The foundation stone speaks for itself:-
"ST. MATTHIAS MISSION CHURCH ERECTED 1891.
FOR THE GLORY OF GOD AND THE INCREASE OF HIS CHURCH".
This is situated in Amity Place and was opened in March 1892 to serve the need of the poorer parishioners who could not afford to pay pew rents. The Mission would appear to have seated about 200 persons. The building is in red brick and has a turret with one bell. Now no longer used for religious purposes, it serves as a depot for a television rental firm. Although its use has been changed, its appearance leaves no doubt as to its former purpose, despite the fact that the small turret (still containing the bell) is liberally decorated with television aerials. One wonders what the original worshippers would have thought of them!

Church of St. Michael, Albert Road, Devonport.

This was built in 1845 at a cost of £5,000 and designed to seat 1,200 persons. Stone for the church was given by the Government from the quarry then existing at Richmond Walk. The parish was created from that of Stoke Damerel.
This was a large church. It had three galleries, one at the west end and one in each of the transepts.
In the 1941 blitz, the building was hit by four bombs and destroyed. Services were transferred to the church hall.
Rebuilding started in 1951, the architects being Messrs. Arthur Martin and Keith Fox. Limestone for the walls came from the blitzed schools of St. James the Less at Millbay and the derelict church of St. George on Stonehouse. When the building was complete, an organ was installed which had previously been in the Church of St. John, Devonport, and this was rebuilt over the north transept with a detached console.
The lectern and sanctuary chair are the sole remaining pieces of furniture from the original church.

Church of St. Michael, West Hoe.

In 1870 the parish of St. James the Less was extended 'to take in under the Hoe and Millbay Docks'. It is assumed that about this time the church of St. Michael was built as a daughter church. This is a small building having seats for 200 persons. It is situated in Central Road, very near Rusty Anchor and the Hoe front.
It was undamaged during the war but its use as a place of worship was discontinued for a time and the building used for an electrical business. Sometime after, however, it was taken back by St. Andrew's and again used as a church, a nearby hall having been used for worship during this interim period.
At present from the outside, we see quite a small building with a red tiled roof and a spire containing one bell. Internally, there are certainly some items of interest. The pews came from Christ Church (formerly in Eton place) and two fine stalls for the clergy from the church of St. Catherine. It has a fine carved pulpit which almost certainly came from one of the large churches. The font is most unusual, actually being a ships binnacle and is most striking as one enters the church. The altar bears an inscription: "In memory of John Richard Middleton, killed on active service March 8th 1945. The gift of his wife".
A Women's Fellowship exists and the church carries out certain Youth and Missionary activities.

The Military Chapel, Devonport.

Also known as the Garrison Chapel, this existed on the western side of the road between Cumberland Gardens and Raglan Barracks. The Plymouth Directory of 1899 notes that "…. It is a spacious building of red brick in an adaption of the Early English style. It consists of nave, chancel, north and south aisles, and possesses ample means of ingress and egress. Erected mainly with a view to utility, it has little claim to beauty".

Personal recollection is that it was a long, low building and mainly served the soldiers at the Raglan and Granby Barracks. It was set back from the road with a strip of grass or lawn in front. Probably used for church parades, hence the 'ample means of ingress and egress' quote above.

Footnote: Devonport Garrison Church damaged during war. Demolished in 1952. Eight 3 bedroom flats designed by Major W.T. Elford erected. Old church foundations said to be able to 'carry a battleship' used for the new buildings. Erected for use of families of the Territorial Army.

Church of St. Nicholas, R.N. Barracks.

Erected in 1907 to the design of Mr. P.J. Marvin, this building can accommodate 900 persons.
A fine rood screen designed by Mr. W.D. Caroe has been installed as a memorial to those men of the Navy who lost their lives in the 1914/18 war.
The altar came from H.M.S. Tiger. Other items of note are the fine lectern and the stained glass windows. The building also contains a silver replica of Drake's Drum as well as a model of H.M.S. Devonshire. A model of the Golden Hind is suspended from the roof of the nave.
Restoration to the church was carried out in 1953.

Parish Church of St. Pancras.

The tything of Weston Peverell or Pennycross goes back to the Normans and the manors of Pennycross are recorded in the Domesdaybook.
The first mention of a chapel at 'Penniecross' is in the 16th century when it is known that it was attached to the manor. It is shown on 'Spry's plot'- an early map - about 1695.
Before 1820 the Tything of Weston Peverell was not a parish in its own right but a chapelry under the control of the Vicar of St.

Andrew's. About 1820 the old chapel was demolished except for the part which now forms the chancel in the present building, the stone from the old being used to form the new. The old font was discarded (probably built into the walls) and the one we now see was brought from St. Budeaux where it had been installed in 1482. It now stands inside the main door and it is of interest to note that it is similar to that at Walkhampton Church.

Mention of Spry's Plot has been made and this is often referred to as being a record of the line of Drakes leat built in 1591. This leat had been cut through the tything and later the Stonehouse leat (1593) and the Devonport leat (1793) were also constructed. The vestry had trouble with all three authorities, mainly regarding roads and bridges; one leat overflowed into Ham Lane in 1843, Devonport was requested to repair the bridge where the leat crossed Ham Lane in 1845, and Stonehouse was asked to remove boundary stones illegally placed on the Pennycross roads in 1848. The route of the leat can still be traced through the graveyard opposite the church and part of one of the granite bridges still exits nearby,

To return to the church itself. Up to 1820 services had been conducted infrequently by the Vicar or Curate of St. Budeaux. Repairs and alterations took place between 1866 and 1870, the building being enlarged and the old horse box pews removed and replaced by more modern ones. The parish was created in 1898. The chalice of St. Pancras (now kept at Buckland Abbey) dates back to 1695, the coat of arms thereon being similar but not identical to those of the Harris family of Radford. The church register records members of the Prouse family being buried in 1637, 1662 and 1675. A coat of arms appears on the stone just at the back of the church in what is now known as Prowse Crescent, and it is of interest to note that this stone also bears the inscription 'H 1792 H' which is thought to refer to Humphrey Hall who possessed Manadon from 1767 to 1787, and was related to Rev. G. Hall-Parlby (see notes on Emmanuel).

In the year 1939 the west end of St. Pancras was damaged and until 1956 services were held at the now demolished St. Martin's Crypt (q.v). Repairs were effected and a piece of marble from St. Paul's Cathedral built into the south wall of the chancel. Since then further modernisation has taken place to the internal arrangements of the church and a fine new wall added.

A church which, in living memory was well out in the country, is now in the centre of a busy and expanding area.

This is a historic building which is well worth a visit.

(Further information)

About 1974 alterations were made to the chancel. All the choir stalls were removed and the screen modified. The pulpit was also taken away.

Apart from strictly religious activities, St. Pancras is also energetic in other ways. Social and communal events take place, the Senior Citizens Club, for instance. A playgroup also exists. Much work is done among the young people of the parish.

Work is also carried on in connection with foreign missions. Close ties also exist with St. Judes.

Parish Church of St. Paul, Stonehouse.

Now properly called 'The Parish Church of St. George with St. Paul' it was originally built as a chapel-of-ease to St. George. It is assumed that the construction of the Royal William Yard, the Royal Marine Barracks and the Royal Naval Hospital caused the area to become more populous, hence the need for this additional place of worship.

St. Paul's was built in 1831 to the design of John Foulston and a parish was formed in 1883. The money to build the church had come partly from private subscription and partly from His Majesty's (William IV) Commissioners for building the new church and the site had been given by the Earl of Mount Edgcumbe and his family.

After the destruction of the church of St. George in April 1941, the two congregations merged and in 1954 became as we have seen, the Church of St. George with St. Paul. It now has no resident priest but is served from St. Andrew's.

St. Paul's, believed to be the last church Foulston built in Plymouth, is of distinguished external appearance, having a square tower and bell which also contains a clock. The tower is surmounted by four pinnacles. Internally the church is rather bare but it has got a balcony on which is affixed the Royal Coat of Arms. Of some note, too, are the carvings on the choir stalls, the carved stone font and the inscription behind the high altar: 'Holy, Holy, Holy, Lord God of Hosts'. Although the church of St. George is no more, it is commemorated by the brass altar cross mounted on a block of stone which is on the side altar of St. Paul's, both the cross and the stone coming from the destroyed church.

In the vestry is preserved an item of considerable interest, fragments of an old pre-Reformation bible. Details noted in relation to this are:

'These two fragments are part of an illuminated pre-Reformation bible which was in use at the Church or Chapel which stood in this place prior to the erection of the present parish church.

The fragments were found during an examination of the old churchwarden's account book which dates from 1574 and deals mainly with the letting of seats in the church. The fragments were used as part of the binding of the account book and are therefore older than 1574 at least.

The subject matter on the pages comprises parts of XXI, XXII, and XXIII chapters of the book of Joshua together with parts I and II chapters of the book of Judges. The illuminated first letter of the first chapter of the book of Judges can be seen (partly) on the right. The language is Latin and in some places is much abbreviated, especially can this be noticed on the other side of the left hand fragment, where the scribe has omitted by mistake verses 34 to 39 of the XXI chapter which caused him to overlook the intervening verses.

When the old Latin service books and bibles were superseded at the Reformation by books written in the English language, they were often cut up and used for all sorts of purposes. Their gold illumination was stripped off and as the vellum or parchment leaves were durable in character, they were used for binding new books. This is evidently what happened in the case of these two fragments. At the foot of the left hand fragment the name 'Edgcumbe' can faintly be seen. In the account book referred to above, there are numerous references to the letting of seats in the old chapel or church to members of that family, indicating the close connections that members of the Mount Edgcumbe family had with the church of East Stonehouse in past days'.

The foregoing is a copy of the descriptive text at St. Paul's relating to this extremely interesting and historic relic of the past.

Stonehouse as part of the City of Plymouth is not very well known, yet its history dates back at least to Norman times. Perhaps we can do no better in ending these notes than quote from the Doomsday Book: "Robert himself holds Stanehus. Alwin held it in the time of King Edward and it paid geld for one ferling. There is land for one plough. There is one villein returning five shillings".

Parish of Emmanuel, Church of St. Paul, Efford.

This is a daughter church of Emmanuel. It has no resident priest but is served from the Mother church.

The hall was built in 1952 (a red brick structure) and the church itself in 1963 at a cost of £30,000 the foundation stone having been laid by the Bishop of Plymouth.

Situated on one of the highest parts of Efford and overlooking the Plym estuary, this is a very modern church which, with its clean lines and functional appearance fits in well with its surroundings.

The Church of St. Paul, Morice Square, Devonport.

Not a great deal is known of this church but the Plymouth Directory of 1899 describes it as in the Decorated style and erected in 1849/50 by public subscription '…..the living is a vicarage in the gift of the Crown and the Bishop of Exeter alternately….' The architect was Piers St. Aubyn.

It is assumed to have been one of the many churches destroyed in the 1941 blitz when the heart of Devonport was gutted, never again to become the thriving and busy place that many of the older people remember.

Church of St. Peter, Wyndham Square.

In 1830, the Rev. John Hawker, curate of Stoke Damerel for 30 years, resigned from that church and he and his followers erected a chapel at Five Fields, Eldad. It is said to have been a very ugly building, with galleries and a three decker pulpit. It was known as 'Mr. Hawker's Chapel' and when he died it fell into disuse.

In 1843 an act permitted the formation of a new parish and in 1848 Hawker's old chapel was purchased and renamed the Church of St. Peter.

At that time there was no other place of worship in the Eldad area except a chapel of the Latter Day Saints which is said to have closed soon after the creation of this new parish.

Hawker's old chapel, now St. Peter's, was altered in 1849 and it is assumed that it was the galleries and three decker pulpit that were removed.

George Rundle Prynne (1808-1903) from Looe became the first vicar and his ministry lasted for 55 years until his death. He was an outstanding man who did much for the moral and physical welfare of the district. In the cholera epidemic of 1849 the death rate was enormous and the Rev. Prynne organised resources to fight the disease. Help was offered him in this work by Miss Lydia Sellon (believed to have been the daughter of Capt. Sellon R.N. who did so much good work in the early days of St. James the Great in Devonport). Miss Sellon (1821-1876) was the foundress and superior of the Society of the Most Holy Trinity and it is of interest to note here that sisters of that Order were associated with Florence

Nightingale during the Crimean War. She (Miss Sellon) purchased houses in Wyndham Square and a plot of ground was bought overlooking the 'Mere' (now Victoria Park). A temporary wooden hospital was quickly erected (later to be replaced by a permanent building which is now St. Dunstan's Abbey, and there is no doubt that much devoted service was rendered by Mr. Prynne, Miss Sellon and her Sisters to fight the terrible plague of cholera.

To return to the present St. Peter's.

In 1850 the chancel was built (architect thought to be Piers St. Aubyn), the nave and chapel being added in 1882 to the design of the vicar's son, Mr. George Fellows Prynne. After the death of Mr. G.R. Prynne in 1903, the copper clad spire was built as a memorial to the man who had given most of his life in serving the Church and in serving others.

St. Peter became the Mother Church of All Saints (parish created in 1867) and of the Good Shepherd in Octagon Street. This latter building no longer is a place of worship but used by a firm supplying electrical goods.

The church of St. Peter, which has been described as '.... built of the native limestone in the Early English cruciform plan, with a Lady Chapel, south porch and western tower....' was partially destroyed in the blitz of 1941. Services were then transferred to a nearby hall (this could have been the large hall at the other end of Wyndham Street which although now used for sporting activities, still carries a faint tracing of crossed keys just below the apex of the roof).

Later, the reconstructed church rose again with the restoration being carried out under the direction of Mr. Frederick Etchells who had been responsible for similar work at St. Andrew's. The church was reconstructed in 1956.

This is now a fine large building, which is much simpler in style internally than it was before the blitz. Much of the former ornamentation has been swept away, the much less elaborate appearance having a dignity and harmony of its own. It has some fine statues, in particular one of the Virgin Mary and another most attractive one of St. Francis of Assisi with the animals. The Stations of the Cross are also of note. These are unusual yet they have a sense of integrity. A triptych from the old church is now in the church of St. Francis at Honicknowle.

Perhaps we should not leave these notes on St. Peter's without speaking of George Rundle Prynne in more detail. He seems to have run into trouble at one time in his belief in the continuity of the Catholic faith within the C of E.

It is believed he is accused of papist practices. There is little doubt, however, that during his long ministry he did much for the spiritual and physical welfare of the parish. He was the composer of the hymn 'Jesu, meek and gentle'. A fine man who died respected by all and he was buried at Plympton church where his headstone can still be seen. He deserves not to be forgotten.

Notes:

Lady altar plus cross from demolished church of St. Matthew, Stonehouse.

In 1899, the Rev. G.R. Prynne abandoned the use of incense in obedience to an appeal by the then Archbishop of Canterbury, Dr Temple. Mr Prynne's Curate, the Rev. H.H. Leeper, then resigned and later became Vicar of St. Stephen's, Devonport.

Mission Church of St. Philip and St. James, Weston Mill.

During the 19th century the Dockyard had been spreading steadily northward along the banks of the Tamar, first by the construction of what was known as the Keyham Steam Yard and at the end of the century, the Keyham Dockyard Extension.

Sir John Jackson who was responsible for this extension, erected many houses for workmen engaged on the project. These were on the north side of Keyham Barton hill, what is now known as the Weston Mill Estate, although some older people still think of it as 'Jackson's Estate'.

To serve the spiritual needs of his employees, Sir John erected two Mission Halls, one in Ocean Street (the forerunner of the Church of

St. Thomas) and the other at the rear of Bridwell Road, also making provision for the stipends for the Chaplains for these two places of worship. He also built a school room at Weston Mill but this closed when the new school was erected at Camel's Head.

Regular services took place at the Bridwell Road Mission. It became known as 'St. Philip and St. James Mission Church' and was licensed for public worship in 1898. Lady Jackson took a great interest in the welfare of the district and provided a Mission room at the top of Bridwell Road.

The Rev. T. Heywood became the Minister of St. Philip and St. James Mission in 1908 and it was during his six years of service there that the new permanent Church of St. Philip came to be built.

The Church of St. Philip, Weston Mill.

As has been previously noted, it was during the ministry of the Rev. T. Heywood at the Mission of St. Philip and St. James that the new church came to be built.

In 1910, plans were invited from Mr. M.A. Bazeley, the site having been generously given by Mr. Richard Hall Clarke of Cullompton. By the end of 1911 £5,000 had been guaranteed for the church, Mr Bazeley's plans accepted and work ordered to be commenced. Messrs. Lapthorn of Plymouth were the contractors and the foundation stone was laid by the Bishop of Exeter in May 1912. By the end of 1913 the building and furnishing was complete as far as the chancel arch and the consecration took place in October of that year. The oak pulpit was given by the vicar and wardens of St. Stephen's, Saltash, and the font by Mr.Bazeley the architect. The organ was lent by Sir John Jackson and this was presented by Lady Jackson after Sir John's death.

A parish was formed in 1933 but during the last war the church became linked with St. Budeaux until 1955 when a vicar was installed.

The chancel was added and a vicarage built in 1960 (ground to the extent of about half an acre had been given in 1919 by Mr. J.W. Clarke, son of R.H. Clarke, for the erection of the vicarage but it was not until 1963 that the east end of the church was finally completed.

It is noted that in the post war era, the lectern from the Church of St. Catherine was obtained by the then vicar, the Rev. R.S. Chalk, and the choir stalls came from St. Luke about 1959/60 when it had been decided to demolish that church (this did not, in fact, take place).

This fine limestone building serves the community well. A noteworthy stained glass window now exists behind the main altar. Back in 1934, a booklet was published dealing with the history of St. Philip's. Noting the work still to be done in the future (Vicarage, completion of building, Church Hall), the account ends:- "Hitherto the Lord hath helped us and, if we do our part, under the guidance of the Holy Spirit, we shall make St. Philip's, Weston Mill, a worthy part of God's Vineyard, the church".

This 1934 aspiration seems to have come to pass.

The Church of St. Saviour.

About 1850, Castle Street had 7 public houses and 5 beer houses and was in an area noted for its debauchery. The street was only 12 feet wide and much overcrowding existed in the 30 houses which made up the street. Although only 12 drinking houses have been noted, a contemporary comment was '…. every house was …. an inn and every inn a brothel….'

Castle Street is said to have housed 564 persons on an average of 19 to a room, and it became known to some as 'Damnation Alley'. This then was the position which faced Parson Barnes of nearby Holy Trinity. A man of character he became the terror of wrongdoers and would roam Damnation Alley breaking up the orgies taking place in the 'bunker' or 'tiddleywink' houses. His efforts were so successful that some of the owners fled.

Parson Barnes seems to have been a man of much determination and no little courage. He caused St. Saviour's to be built about 1851. An early account notes that '…. the Parish was formed in 1883 from that of Holy Trinity and in that year the church was enlarged by the addition of the north aisle. Situated on Lambeth Hill near the Citadel. Of stone in the Early English style it has chancel, nave, aisles and a western tower. 530 sittings'.
The building still exists although it is no longer used as a church. Standing now amid modern housing, Parson Barnes' squat limestone tower still dominates Castle Street.
Note: See also Holy Trinity.

Church of St. Simon.

A fine limestone building of which the foundation stone was laid in 1905 by the Archbishop of Canterbury. The church was consecrated in 1907 and in the same year it became a parish created out of that of St. Jude to serve the Mount Gould and Lipson areas. The Parish hall had been built in 1903 and the temporary west wall was made permanent in 1957. Described as being in the Perpendicular style, it has a crypt in which the choir vestry is situated. Said to seat 700.
The three manual organ came from a church in Norwich and a vicarage has been added in 1963.
It is thought that only the base of the northwest tower is complete.

Church of St. Stephen, George Street, Devonport.

Built in 1850 to the design of Mr. Piers St. Aubyn, it is described in an early report as being '…. in the Decorated style and the decorations are elaborate….' Photographs which still exist show it to have been a large three aisled church with considerable ornamentation.
Before the last war (about 1919) a crucifix was erected as a war memorial to the fallen by the priest in charge, Rev. H.H. Leeper.

This memorial was outside the church at the north east corner. Regrettably, Father Leeper had not obtained a faculty for its erection from the Diocese of Exeter and its presence met with some local opposition. Demonstrations were held (probably by members of the Kensit Party who were not noted for their tolerance), letters were written to the paper and general unpleasantness - probably from a small minority - ensued. The crucifix was taken down and sent for storage to the premises of the firm at Cattedown which had been responsible for its construction.

During the last war the Church of St. Stephen was destroyed in the blitz of 1941. At about the same time, the works at Cattedown where the crucifix had been stored were also hit. Later this memorial was found floating in the Sound and rescued, the wood in it being used to make a smaller crucifix and a carving of St. Stephen. Both these items now form part of the Altar of St. Stephen which exists at the Church of St. James the Less at Ham. It is good to think that a little of the old Church of St. Stephen in Devonport (well remembered by many older people) still remains, although the site at the junction of Clowance Street and George Street is now covered by a block of flats and no trace of the church can be seen.

Note: Father Leeper had been a curate at St. Peter's during the time of Father Prynne - he left to become vicar of St. Stephen's (not agreeing with the abandoning of incense by Mr. Prynne).

Parish Church of Stoke Damerel.

This is one of the most interesting churches in the City and perhaps to start these notes we can do no better than quote from the abbreviated details displayed outside the south entrance:

"Diocese of Exeter
The Parish Church of Stoke Damerel
St. Andrew and St. Mary

Here stands a church where a church has stood for the greater part of a thousand years.

Remnants of an earlier building may be seen in the tower, the archway in the north wall, and in the north porch.
The main structure belongs to the years 1700 - 1800 and many of the interior features tell the story behind that period of reconstruction, the need for a larger church to accommodate the many people who made their homes in this ancient parish, with the development of the naval establishment and the coming of the Royal Dockyard.
The roof is supported by ships pillars and an interesting assortment of ships fitments are incorporated in the building.
But through all the changes of time, the purpose of the building has remained unchanged.
 It is the House of God.
 We invite you to worship here."
The derivation of Stoke (the old Stoches) seems to come from one definition of it as a 'fortified place'. Before the Conquest the manor was held by a Saxon named Brismar. After the Conquest the manor was given to one Robert d'Albemarle, and it is easy to see how 'Stoches d'Albemarle' became Stoke Damerel.
There is evidence that a church existed here in the 13th century and at that time it was in a very isolated position overlooking the creek which ran into Stonehouse Pool. The creek ran right up to Pennycomequick, parts of it being known as Deadlake and The Mere. That part above Millbridge was filled in about the end of the last century (now Victoria Park) and the lower part towards Stonehouse has only been filled in recent years to become an open space.
No traces of the 13th century church can be seen but there are still parts of the 15th century building to be observed in the tower and in the porches. Worth's History of Devonport notes:- "A couple of rude granite heads - relics of the old church - the carving of which resembles that of the crosses so common in Cornwall and which appear to be referable to the same period as the memorials, are built into the piers of the churchyard. One with a beard by the saltaire

below would seem to be St. Andrew; the other, a female, is probably intended for the Virgin Mary, the emblem below resembling a double fleur de lis. Possibly they represent the patron saints".

The stone carvings mentioned in the passage above were removed from the outside of the church in 1973 and are now in the south porch and it is thought that Worth was right in that they do represent St. Andrew and the Virgin Mary and that this may have been the original dedication of the church.

In 1690 the Naval Base was started in Dock (later Devonport) and the district became more populous, so much so that the population exceeded that of Plymouth and 'Plymouth Dock' became Devonport in 1824. Early in the 18th century the building had been enlarged and in 1750 it was made bigger again. A request for financial assistance was made to the Admiralty but although this was not forthcoming certain materials for the church were made available; ship's knees, beams and spars were used to reconstruct the roof, the supporting pillars of which were ship's masts. Cabin doors and fanlights were employed and much of this can still be seen.

Formerly the church had a gallery (removed in 1873) and the box pews were replaced by chairs in 1883. The gas lighting which had been installed in 1813 was replaced by electricity in 1911.

The clock was put into the tower in 1811 and had an unusual feature in that it employed a 1½ second pendulum. Signed on the setting dial is 'John Pollard of Plymouth Dock' and the inscription under the face reads 'this clock was erected in 1811, Richard Rodd and Geo. Snowden, Churchwardens'.

In 1553 the tower had four bells but in 1789 these were recast by Bilbie and made into a peal of six. No.6, the tenor bell and the largest, weighed about 14cwts. They were rehung in 1923 - 24. At the end of July 1977 the six bells were removed and sent to Whitechapel for recasting into a peal of eight smaller bells and at the same time the clock slightly modified to accommodate the new peal. The work of removal of these bells in 1977 was carried out in the main by parishioners, a considerable undertaking which shows what can be done by voluntary and willing help. Before the despatch of these bells to Whitechapel, the details were noted. On the tenor bell was seen: 'TO THE CHURCH THE LIVING CALL AND TO THE GRAVE DO SUMMON ALL' and below this 'Mr. James Hore. Mr. Ralph May. Churchwardens', and finally the maker's name: T. Bilbie. Fecit 1789. All bells carried the maker's name and in addition No.5 had: 'GOD SAVE THE KING'.

Still with the bells - The 1789 peal was first used as King George III drove by to visit Plymouth Dock in that year and a rhyme on the tower wall commemorates this occasion:-

"Let awful silence first among us reign.
Then let this useful Law each one maintain.
We ring the Quick to Church, the dead to the grave.
Our use is good, such usage let us have;
We swear or curse, or yet in Angry Mood.
Quarrel or Strike (although he draws no blood).
Wears Hat, Boot, Spur, or overturn a Bell,
Or by unskillful handling Mars a peal.
Let him pay sixpence for each single crime.
To make him cautious on another time.
When 'tis the Sexton's fault to cause delay
We call from him a Double Penalty.
May Concord Reign among us as we Ring.
Pray God preserve our Country, Church and King,
On whose account these Bells were first rung here
When George our King did in the West appear."

It is hoped the bells will be returned after re-casting at the end of this year (1977).

The churchyard has a varied history. Many victims of the cholera epidemics of 1832 and 1849 were buried here; in 1788 a Dockyard clerk was murdered inside the churchyard walls, and it certainly was a happy hunting ground (perhaps not a very apt expression!) for body snatchers, who, after dis-interring the corpses, would transport them to Deadlake and row them out to a waiting barge. It would appear to have been a highly lucrative, if somewhat gruesome, trade. In 1860, under the heading of 'Disgraceful Conduct' it was reported that a man had been seen cutting the grass in the burial ground on a Sunday evening. He said he had paid six shillings to the Sexton for the right to do this, the grass being to feed his donkey. It is understood that the donkey had nothing to say!

The former burial ground is now a public open space with most of the headstones placed round the walls or laid out as paths. It has now been taken over by the City Council who are responsible for its upkeep.

The church itself is rich in monuments. One memorial to Admiral Bacon is tastefully decorated with skulls and surmounted by a pig. Perhaps his descendants had a sense of humour.

During the last war the building suffered no major damage, in fact, it was the only Devonport church to escape. In one of the windows is preserved the brass cross from the altar of St. Luke, Richmond Walk, which had been totally destroyed by enemy action at this time.

In 1894 the rector was the Rev. Gordon Ponsonby, who in 1900 decided to build a new Rectory in the Valletort area not far from Nelson Gardens. It was also intended to build the new Devonport Cathedral there. The foundation stone (now preserved in the South Porch) for the cathedral was laid in 1902 and the Lady Chapel, Crypt and Vestries built (Architect: Mr Caroe). No further building was ever carried out but that already existing was dedicated to St. Mary and used for services. Later services were discontinued and it was used as a church hall, and later still it is thought to have been used by a film company. It was demolished about 1964 and the ground sold. The Rectory, now known as Collingwood House, still remains and is used as accommodation under the control of the city.

A short account cannot do justice to this interesting and outstanding church. An excellent booklet written by Patricia Gray does exit and makes fascinating reading. I have drawn freely on this account. With the booklet as a guide, a visit to the Church of Stoke Damerel would be a memorable event.

Omitted in the foregoing account.

Mention should be made of the Furneaux memorial outside the north door. Capt. Tobias Furneaux lived at Swilly House and was an associate of Capt. Cook. Although Swilly House no longer exists, Furneaux Road is named after the occupant and is on the same site, in fact, stone pillars from the boundary walls of this residence still can be seen in the area.

The organ was originally in the gallery but was moved to its present position when the gallery came down in 1873. Rebuilt and altered in 1884, it is now (1977) undergoing repairs through being damaged by water following the theft of lead from the roof.

One of the interesting modern additions is the collection of kneelers. These have been made recently and are still being made. Beautifully worked, they are the efforts of dedicated members of the congregation - the skill and craftsmanship which has gone into them being in great contrast to some of the shoddy massed produced articles of the present day.

Church of St. Thomas the Apostle, Keyham.

A corrugated iron shed-like structure was erected in Fleet Street (near the site of the present church) in 1900 and became known as the Church of the Good Shepherd. This was a daughter church of St. Mark's in Ford.

In 1907 a foundation stone for the new church was laid by Lady St. Levan. In 1908 the building was complete and was dedicated to St. Thomas the Apostle. The old iron (it was probably iron and fibre board) structure continued to be used as a church hall until it was demolished in 1977. The parish had been created in 1929 and a new vicarage constructed about 1950 on a site adjoining the old hut.

A fine church which appears somewhat unfinished at the north east corner. It may have been that a chapel which was in the original design has not yet been built.

Notes: It is noted that Sir John Jackson built 2 mission halls - one at Weston Mill and one in Ocean Street, and it is this one which is said to be the forerunner of St. Thomas. Sir John Jackson was responsible for the Keyham extension of the Yard in the last century.

Mission of St. Thomas.

This is a small red brick building and still exists (although not used for religious purposes now) in Palace Street.

The stone over the door gives us some of the history:- "St. Thomas's Mission Chapel. Parish of St. Andrew. Erected to the memory of John Kelly, twice Mayor of Plymouth, by Mrs. John Kelly, 1885".

Another Mission at which the Rev. R.S. Chalk remembers an active congregation.

NON CONFORMIST CHURCHES.
General.

Back in 1662, many ministers were ejected from their livings because they would not conform to the policies of the Church of England.

In 1664 the Conventicle Act was passed which made it illegal for more than five persons to meet (in addition to the family of the house in which they were gathering) for religious purposes not in accordance with the C of E prayer book.

During this period, non-conformist meetings were held, sometimes in the open and sometimes in private houses, but always at the risk of prosecution. They met at their peril and many suffered for it.

In 1689 came the Toleration Act which allowed dissenting Ministers to hold services on certain conditions, and following this, many churches and meeting houses were erected. Sometimes those of different denominations met together, and it is said that it was a Company of Baptists, Congregationalists, Quakers and Unitarians who extended their hospitality to the Pilgrim Fathers, who are reported as having been 'courteously used and kindly entertained'. Very different is the situation now when churches of all denominations are co-operating; C of E with R.C, Methodists with Baptists and so on. Nothing but good can come of this and as has been said:- "God has many names but there is only on God".

BAPTIST

Crownhill Baptist Church

This stems from the old Pembroke Street, Devonport church (q.v) which had been purchased by the corporation in 1953 for the construction of flats when the area was re-planned. The money received in compensation covered the erection of the new church at Crownhill.

Foundation stones were laid on 25th May, 1957, one by Mr. Edwin S. Williams and another which reads: 'To the Glory of God and to commemorate the church at Pembroke Street, founded 1789 now continued here, this stone was laid by the Senior Member, Mrs. Florence M. Coram on the twenty fifth of May 1957'. Mrs Coram had been a lifelong member of the Devonport church. The ceremony was also attended by the Minister, Mr. Dyer. A photo of the event shows Mrs. Coram's grandson, then a young boy, who it is expected will be ordained this year (1977).

This is a modern church and community unit. The building occupies an excellent position amid a housing estate and its somewhat squarish appearance is enhanced by the entrance porch and the small spire which surmounts the roof.

Close ties exist with the Mutley Baptist Church.

Note: David Coram is being ordained as Baptist Minister at an ordination service to be held at Old George Street, Baptist Church on 15th September 1977. This will be followed by an induction service at Okehampton Baptist Church on 17th September where he will become the new Pastor.

Efford Baptist Church.

Owing to the growth of this district in post war years, a Plymouth Corporation nissen hut was used in 1948 for religious services and for a Sunday school. Although at first attendances were small, the work went ahead. Much help was given by the Hope Baptist Church at Peverell.
In 1950 larger premises were secured and a lay Pastor appointed. Later, a Deaconess was given overall charge and new premises known as 'Church House' were used.
The present buildings were erected in 1960 and the services of a full time Minister were employed.
It is understood that the war damage payment from the blitzed Ebenezer Baptist Church which had existed in Union Street enabled the present Efford church to come into being.

Emmanuel Baptist Church, North Road, Plymouth.

This a red brick fronted structure with a small tower and a copper clad spire.
The pediment over the main door is of some note. It takes the form of a triangular carving, possibly in sandstone, in the centre of which is an open book inscribed 'God with us' surmounted by a dove. The date 1899 also appears and at the bottom of the carving the words: 'Emmanuel Chapel'. An unusual carving which must have been un-noticed by many who pass.
On one side of the main door is a stone: 'Wiblin and de Bonneville, Architects, J. Paynter, Builder' and on the other side of the entrance is a badly weathered stone, the inscription being in places indecipherable. It reads: 'To the Glory of God …. une Jehovah.

This stone was laid on behalf of Trustees and Congregation (Trinity?) York Street. 1899'. A list of names then follows.
One account notes that the church was built in 1864 and seated 300 – it is thought that this must have referred to another building which possibly existed before the present one.

Estover Baptist Church.

Biscuits. It seems strange to start a description of the origins of a church by talking about biscuits but there is some connection.
In 1830 a Mr. Frean bought premises at Lambhay and started to manufacture biscuits. He was joined by a Mr. Daw and a Mr. Serpell, flour millers at Drake's Mill, Sherwell. Robert Serpell became the surviving partner and he was followed by his son, Henry Serpell. In 1899 the whole business was transferred to Reading and only in recent years have the names of Serpell and Frean (Peak Frean) become less well known.
Henry Serpell lived at Estover and as a further digression, the Concise Oxford Dictionary defines 'Estovers' as: 'Necessaries allowed by law as wood allowed for repairs or fuel taken by a tenant from his holding'. In view of the fact that there were extensive woods nearby, is there any connection? To return to Henry Serpell, he was a Deacon of George Street Baptist Church and knowing the need for a place of worship in his own area, started holding services at his home, Estover House. The numbers grew and the accommodation became inadequate, so proceedings were started to enable a permanent church to be built. A Mr. Charles Norrington, the owner of Estover Quarries, gave the site but insisted that the church when it was built should be undenominational.
The church was erected with stone from Mr. Norrington's quarry and the first trustees included Anglicans, Baptists, Congregationalists, Wesleyans and Quakers.
When Mr. Serpell died, a Mr. Cole - a Methodist - took over the responsibility for running the church and it remained this way until

1945 when Mr. A.B. Pendock, a Baptist, took over. Mr. Pendock continued as Lay Pastor until his death in 1976.

Notable persons in connection with the conduct of the church in the past are the Deacons in charge, Mr. D. Mountford, Mr. G. Gorman and Miss P. Trounson.

For many years until his death in 1976, the church was fortunate in having the services of Mr. E. Folley as Lay Reader. Mr. Folley was born at Roborough Reservoir and had lived in the Glenholt area for about 50 years. He was a man of great integrity whose upright living and undoubted probity had made him well respected in the district. At his funeral the Minister remarked that it was not so much a case of the world having suffered a loss as the fact that the world was a better place for his having been here - sentiments with which all knew him would agree.

Estover church has seen many changes. Originally in an isolated country district, it is now in the middle of an industrial estate and near the City Airport. Lighting was formally by oil, then acetylene (this had a habit of giving trouble in the middle of a service) and now by electricity. The organ is said to have come from a north country mansion and had no doubt been acquired by Mr. Serpell during his business travels.

For many years Estover has had close ties with Hope Baptist at Peverell.

Not a large church but one that still preserves the country atmosphere and still serves the district well.

Ford Baptist Church

This is said to have been started by three members of Hope Baptist (q.v). In 1863 a room was rented in Emma Cottages, Seaton Place, Ford, on premises owned by a Mr. Blatchford, a dairy man.

The cause prospered and within a year larger premises were required. Mr. Blatchford, who was building some houses nearby, modified one of them to provide a large room - a whole floor - for rental by the congregation. Later, a plot of ground (that on which the school now stands), was purchased for £60. Worship continued, however, in the large room and in 1866 a Sunday School was started.

In 1868 a new chapel was opened on the £60 site and extensions made to this building in 1882. It was becoming apparent, however, that the need for a larger church existed and in 1898 foundation stones were laid for the new building (the present one) immediately above the old chapel. The new church to hold 480 persons was opened in 1899 and the buildings on the lower site then used as a school.

At this point the Rev. A.T. Head should be mentioned. He commenced his ministry at Ford in 1878 and his devoted service lasted until 1917 when he resigned his Pastorate. Still remembered by many older people, a brass plate in the church now commemorates this well loved minister.

Many notable persons have been connected with Ford: Mr. R.C. Serpell, Mr. Henry Hurrell, Alderman J.T. Bond (whose name is still seen on boundary stones and was Mayor at the time of the completion of Burrator Reservoir) and many others. It was Mr. Bond who gave the original organ, replaced by a pipe organ in 1907.

The church has been in constant use up to the present day - even during the blitz when the roof had been badly damaged by fire bombs. It has an active religious and social life and maintains ties of fellowship with other churches in the St. Levan Valley.

A point of interest is that the granddaughter of Rev. A.T. Head is a devoted worker for the church, a church which owed so much in the beginning to the generous help and interest of George Street, Mutley and Hope Baptists congregations.

George Street, Baptist

One cannot think about the beginning of this church without the name of Abraham Cheare coming to mind. In the days of religious intolerance, Cheare, who seems to have been a fearless man, suffered much. He was imprisoned at Exeter and later in the dungeons at Drake's Island where he died at the age of 42. He was first appointed minister in 1648 and was closely associated with the church which we now know as George Street Baptist. Because of intolerance, the Pilgrim Fathers left the country to obtain freedom and during their 1620 stay in Plymouth before setting out, they are said to have been 'courteously used and kindly entertained' hospitality having been extended to them by a company of Baptists, Congregationalists, Quakers and Unitarians'.

In 1649 premises known as the Pig Market Meeting House were used as a Baptist chapel and this served until the congregation moved to larger premises in How Street in 1789. In 1797, a site, approximately where the Council House now stands, was purchased and a beautiful church which would hold 1,000 persons was built and opened in 1845. Many older people will remember this building which stood behind the old George Street and was not visible from the main road. In 1899 the interior of the church was reconstructed and the building remained until being destroyed by the blitz of 1941. In some pictures of the church a tree is visible which was known by some as 'the tree of life', and this may well be one of the trees which still exist outside the present Council buildings.

When the new City Centre was designed after the war, the destroyed church was not re-erected on the same site but on one below the City Treasury and near the Synagogue in Catherine Street, but still retains the name of George Street Baptist Church. In the interim period between the destruction of the old church and the building of the new, services were conducted at the Mutley Baptist Church, the Lower Street Mission and in 1946 at the Catholic Apostolic Church (built 1867) in Princess Street.

The new church was built in 1958, the foundation stone having been laid by Lady Astor in 1957. As one enters the church now, two stones of note can be seen outside the porch on the left hand side. One reads: 'Founded 1620. The church situated in George Street was built in 1845 and destroyed in March 1941', and the other: 'This Remembrance stone was recovered from the ruins of the building in George Street and laid on 2nd November, 1957, by John Cottrell, Secretary'.

From the outside the present building has a good appearance. The roof is surmounted by a short octagonal tower over which is an unusual twisted spire supported on eight pillars, this slender spire being crowned by a metal cross.

Inside, the church is light and spacious with a gallery at the rear. The focal point is, however, the fine mural depicting the baptism of Our Lord which is seen on the front internal wall. Many consider this mural to be quite outstanding.

In its long and interesting history of over 350 years the Baptist congregation has met in a number of locations, but throughout all this time the principles of sincere worship have remained unchanged.

Hope Baptist Church.

In 1852 the Rev. Thomas Horton who had been minister at Morice Baptist Church for 31 years, left that church with 150 members of the congregation and moved to a chapel in Mount Street, Devonport. In 1855 they moved again to the Hope Baptist chapel in Fore Street. School rooms were erected nearby in 1869 - these are believed to have been in Cherry Garden Street, later known as York Street, Devonport.

The Rev. Edward Francis stressed to the Admiralty in 1898 that serving members of the Forces had a right to attend churches of their own denomination and subsequently this point was conceded. In 1924, members of Hope moved to the Peverell area, services being held in Pounds House. The old Fore Street premises were sold to the Wesleyans and they became Central Hall.

The congregation of Hope Baptist Church erected a school hall in Peverell Park Road in 1926.

Mr. Henry Hurrell gave a site for a new church and the foundation stone was laid in 1926. The stone bears a quotation from the 127th

Psalm: 'Except the Lord build the house, they labour in vain that build it'. this extract also appears cut into the granite of Smeaton's lighthouse, now on the Hoe. The church was opened in 1926.
This is a good limestone building standing in a prominent position at the Pennycross end of Peverell Park Road. Recently in 1977, it has been re-roofed and in so doing a large cross has been created on the southern side of the roof by using light coloured tiles.
This is an active church which besides its vigorous religious observances, has also a thriving social life.
Notes: Organ built about 1880 by Hele & Co. Originally in the Devonport church. Re-installed at Peverell by Hele & Co. Alterations plus additions made from time to time. 1975/76 again overhauled and re-furbished.

Morice Baptist Church.

In 1789 the Rev. Isaiah Birt, then minister of Pembroke Street Chapel, obtained former Methodist premises in Morice Square and on the 25th February 1798 the chapel was opened with the Rev. W. Steadman as the first minister. The Morice Square church served the district well until it was destroyed in 1941. Members met in various places of worship until 1949, when 20 of the congregation under Mr. W.G. Randall of St. Budeaux met for services at the Trelawney Secondary Modern School. A foundation stone was laid in May, 1953, and the building (on a site in Ham Drive which had been purchased in 1946) consisting of a new hall and classrooms was opened in 1954. Increasing numbers necessitated extra accommodation so members of the church, helped by a local builder, a Mr. M. Handley, erected a hall to seat 120 and this was opened in 1959.
!960, and the men of the congregation again busy on the church itself. Foundations were laid and the work then handed over to Messrs. E.B.C. & Sleeman, of Exeter for completion.
Those concerned with the erection of the new building included: Mr. Richard Fraser, A.R.I.B and Mr. B.A. Searle of Messsrs. Louis

de Soissons, Messrs. Godfrey Smith and Partners, Messrs E.B.C. Sleeman, Ltd, Mr. S. Mountford and some others.

The opening of the new church was performed by a former Minister, the Rev. Gwynfryn C. Thomas. Those attending included many ministers and representatives of church organisations, Civic leaders, the Architect and officials of the congregation.

At the ceremony, the Architect presented the key to the church Secretary, Mr. P.P. Glanville, who handed it to the Rev. Thomas and the door was unlocked. Thus after 21 years the Morice Baptist church had a new home.

Architecturally, this is an unusual building as the roof is supported by four pillars, the walls themselves carrying only the windows which surround the top of the structure. The interior has a very pleasing, modern look and it seems that its appeal comes from its simplicity. It contains a small balcony. Recreational and other facilities are provided by adjoining buildings.

Mutley Baptist Church.

Owing to the expansion of the town northwards it was realised in the 1860's by the congregation of George Street Baptist Church that another building was desirable. A suitable site was acquired on Mutley Plain and in February 1867 it was decided "to raise the means for the erection of a commodious chapel".

The present church was built and opened in 1869. At this time, the Mutley church was still part of St. George but in 1876 it was agreed that Mutley should become a separate entity, and this it did, the first pastor in that year being the Rev. Benwell Bird from Birmingham. During Mr. Bird's 23 years of ministry, the church prospered and he made valuable and enduring contributions to the creation of real fellowship between various sections of the Christian Church in Plymouth, endearing himself to Anglicans, Catholics and Free Churchmen alike. It was during Mr. Bird's pastorate that new classrooms were erected and later, in 1907 during the ministry of the Rev. J. Bell Johnston that the Caretaker's Cottage, the Spurgeon Hall and other additions were made.

During the last war, although the building was hit by incendiaries and suffered some damage from blast, it never received a direct hit from H.E. bombs and happily did not suffer any major effects. The caretakers of the church and school had promptly dealt with the fire bombs.

After the fall of France in 1940 Plymouth had become the prime target of aerial attacks and many churches and public buildings were destroyed. Consequently, the school hall and certain classrooms were requisitioned by Government Departments. This did mean that some of the weekday activities of the church were curtailed but Sunday services continued.

So many of our Plymouth churches either suffered severe damage or were practically demolished at this time that it was fortunate that Mutley Baptist was able to extend its hospitality to some of the others to enable their services to continue; a truly charitable gesture.

At the present time (1977) certain extensions are being made; it is thought these are in connection with social and youth activities.

Finally, Mutley Baptist Church, with its two towers (said to have a Palladian facade) is a landmark in the City. It now stands in the centre of a busy shopping area - a direct contrast to the scene over 100 years ago when it was built, the district then being almost completely rural with the South Devon Railway cutting only having been made a few years before. Times change but the work and need of the church goes on.

Pembroke Street, Baptist Church.

At the end of the 18th century, Devonport (the Plymouth Dock) was becoming more populous on account of the growth of the Dockyard which had been commenced in 1690.

A Baptist Mission existed in the Pig Market, Plymouth, and it was decided that the need for another meeting house in Devonport should be met. To this end, premises were secured in 1779 at Liberty Street (later Prembroke Street) and until 1789 the mission built here was under the care of the parent church. In this year (1789) it was resolved to form a separate community which became 'The District and Independent Baptist Church' and the first minister after becoming independent was the Rev. Isaiah Birt. The congregation grew so much that the services of an additional minister, the Rev. W. Steadman, became necessary.

Mr. Birt purchased a former Methodist chapel in Morice Square and when this was opened as a Baptist Church, Mr. Birt remained at Liberty Street, and Mr. Steadman took over at Morice Square. Devonport was thus fortunate in having the services of two such excellent ministers.

To revert to Pembroke Street. In 1806 a Sunday School was formed and used premises in Pipe Lane, which ran off Pembroke Street and parallel to James Street. This was the first such school in Devonport.

A noteworthy person was Samuel Nicholson. A member of Pembroke Street Chapel, he preached his first sermon at Millbrook before he was 19 years of age, and went on to become the Pastor of the Plymouth How Street Chapel. It was during his ministry that the George Street Baptist Church (q.v) was built in 1845.

It was in 1897 that the premises in Pembroke Street were rebuilt and at this time heating apparatus was installed and a pipe organ fitted.

The 150th anniversary was celebrated in 1929, those taking part in this event including the Rev. Wilkinson Riddle (from George Street) and Mr. Henry Hurrell, J.P.

In 1953 the Pembroke Street premises were purchased by Plymouth Corporation for the erection of flats in connection with City re-planning and the old building which had served so well was no more.

A new site in the same area was not allocated so with the funds received as compensation a new church was built at Crownhill in 1958. This new building does contain the organ and pulpit from

Pembroke Street. It is said to be thriving and hopes are that it shall soon be extended.

Pembroke Street Baptist Church served well for a period of over 170 years, but it assumed that with the town spreading outwards and with less density of population, the change had to come and transfer to another district inevitable.

As a postscript and for those who remember old Devonport, the location of the chapel was on the left hand side of Pembroke Street going downwards just past Canterbury Street. It was near a boot repair shop run by a Jew named Bence and next door to the chapel lived a noted Plymouth boxer, Len Harvey. Despite the fact that the area was known as 'China Town' many older people recall it with affection.

Notes: see notes on George Street and on Morice Square churches

Salisbury Road Baptist Church.

A site was bought in 1897 by the George Street church, the building erected and opened in 1907. Formerly, services in the area had been held in the council school.

Bombed and damaged by enemy action in 1943, services were again held in the Council School and later in some rooms under the damaged church.

A new hall was built in 1951 and the church rebuilt in 1958 at a cost of £43,000 (the 1907 cost had been between £9,000 - £10,000). The present building is of dressed limestone and has a small tower. One stone in the foundation notes: 'Built of the foundation of the Apostles and Prophets, Himself being the Chief Corner Stone', and another 'To the Glory of God the first church on this site was opened January 20th 1907 and was destroyed by enemy action June 13th 1943. This stone was laid by the Rev. Charles Dyer July 24th, 1957'.

This is a fine large church in a district which has seen much extension to the east in the 1920/1930 years and again in the post war era.

St. Budeaux Baptist Church.

Services commenced in 1899 in a hall over a stable in Yeoman's Terrace (it is assumed that these were premises recently vacated by the Church of England Mission which later became the Church of St. Boniface). The early work in this area was pioneered by members of the Morice Baptist Church in Devonport.

In 1902 a new building was constructed on a site in the main road just below St. Budeaux Square. This served as both a church and a school until 1963 until the opening of the new building nearby. The old premises were then converted to a garage which still retains evidence of its former use.

The new church in Fletemoor Road was commenced in 1961. The foundation stone reads: 'To the Glory of God, this stone was laid on behalf of the Church and Congregation by the Pastor, Rev. Abraham Cutts in June, 1961'.

The present building is modern in appearance with a pillared portico and a copper roof surmounted by a small metal cross. The welfare of the congregation has not been forgotten as a notice is seen outside stating that a nursery is provided for babies and young children during morning services - a practical touch which it is certain will be appreciated.

Other Baptist Places of Worship.

Other meeting places are said to have been at:-

Ebenezer Baptist Chapel, Union Street, Stonehouse. (this would appear to be the first Baptist congregation in Stonehouse).

West Hill Baptist Mission Room, Lipson.

Baptist Mission Hall, Harbour Avenue, Plymouth.

Portland Chapel, Portland Villas, Plymouth.

METHODIST CHURCHES

Compton Methodist Church.

Before the turn of the century, a Methodist community existed in the Compton area and met in a private house in Lower Compton. In 1900 a permanent church was built, one of the outer walls being left unfinished for further possible extension.
In 1939 a completely new church was erected on adjoining land and the old building, now no longer used as a church, serves as a Sunday School and for other activities.
The present Compton Methodist Church is a daughter of Mutley Methodist (now regrettably closed this year – 1977). Situated at the junction of Eggbuckland Road and Revell Road, it is a well built red brick building which will hold several hundred persons. Has an attractive interior with an excellent organ. Small meeting rooms beneath the church itself play an active part in the social and communal life of the district.

Devonport Methodist Central Hall.

A the top of Fore Street, Devonport, the Temperance Hall was built in 1850 and the adjoining premises, next to the still existing public house, became Hope Baptist Chapel in 1855. Later the Temperance Hall became the Sailors and Soldiers Home known as the 'Welcome' (well remembered by many older Devonport people who attended entertainment there). In 1926 the Hope Baptist members moved to Peverell and the premises were purchased by the Wesleyans. This then became the Methodist Central Hall. Both the Welcome and Central Hall were destroyed in the 1941 blitz and a fine new Central Hall with which is associated the Welcome Sunday School and Club rooms commenced in 1956. (As far as can be remembered, the Welcome had continued to function in the interim period in a Nissen hut at the corner of Fore

Street/Marlborough Street before that part was taken over by the Dockyard).

The foundation stone of the new Hall notes that it was laid by Councillor W.J. Oats on 27th October 1956.

The Central Hall itself is an excellent building and contains a good organ. It is an active centre of Methodist religious life in Devonport and, with its ancillary club rooms and other facilities, is a useful addition to communal and social life of the west end of the City.

Plymouth Methodist Central Hall.

Methodists originally met in Plymouth in a private house in Mud Lane, the Mud Street church dating from 1792. In 1816 Ebenezer (later to become the Central Hall) was built on land which was at this time outside the Old Town Gate. This ground was formerly owned by Sir Francis Drake whose name and signature appears on the Deed. At the time of building (but not found until much later) a glass container was embodied in the structure which gave the names of the trustees at the time and also another record which read: 'These premises were bought on March XV MDCCCXVI of Commissioner Fanshawe of the Dock Yard, by Thomas Tanner, Baker, Treville Street, and Richard Lethbridge, Baker and Grocer, Old Town Street, Plymouth, for the purpose of building a Methodist Chapel on. Ebenezer Lethbridge, son of the above Richard Lethbridge, born March 17th, 1866'.

As a digression at this point, it would appear that Commissioner Fanshawe of the Dockyard was not adverse to selling land for a non conformist chapel, despite his threats to discharge Dockyard workers if they continued to attend the Unitarian Chapel in Devonport!

To return to Ebenezer. In 1858, school premises and Ministers' houses were added, some of these additions later becoming shops in the now demolished Saltash Street. Further additions were made in 1892, lecture and class rooms also being added in 1908. At this time Ebenezer was approached through iron gates on Saltash Street, and is shown in an old photo to have had trees in front, in the position now occupied by the car park.

In Ebrington Street nearby stood the Wesleyan Chapel erected in 1877. It was gutted by a disastrous fire in 1937 and the homeless congregation joined those of Ebenezer, which was subsequently modernised, given a 'face lift' inside and out and opened in 1940 as the Plymouth Methodist Central Hall. (it should be mentioned that it was during the 1939/40 'face lift' that the glass container previously mentioned, came to light).

Portions of the old Ebenezer can still be seen although the galleries which existed on three sides of the building have been replaced by one only at the rear. The modified building is said to hold 1,000 persons.

During the last war, despite the severe damage to surrounding property, the Central Hall escaped almost unscathed. It played a great part in the Civic life during this period, being much in demand for official functions, our Guildhall having been destroyed. Since the war many changes have taken place in the area. The Old Drake Circus and Saltash Street have gone; and where formerly the Central Hall faced onto a narrow street, it now occupies a prominent position near the Drake Circus traffic roundabout.

Added in recent years, too, is a small chapel on the Cornwall Street side, a large car park, and a new block containing a large hall, recreation rooms and coffee bar open in 1970.

The Central Hall has served the City well. During the war used for Mayor choosing ceremonies and speech days, now a centre for Methodist religious and social life in Plymouth – a fine record of 150 years.

Footnote: Tablet in Foyer:
'To the Glory of God this tablet was unveiled by the Rev. W.E. Chivers. B.A. commemorating the fusion of the Ebenezer and Wesleyan Congregations to establish the Plymouth Central Hall, 1st

May, 1940. By this union the noble traditions of the two churches are combined to extend the work of God in this City.
'HE HATH MADE OF TWAIN ONE'.
Ebenezer founded 1816. Wesley founded. 1879'.

Another tablet:
'To the Glory of God and in recognition of the close association of the PLYMOUTH CITY COUNCIL and METHODIST CENTRAL HALL 1941- 1949, while the Guildhall was unusable through enemy action. Unveiled September 4th, 1960. Alderman F.J. Stott, J.P. Lord Mayor'.
Regrettably, Mr. Stott died 1st October, 1977.

Ford Methodist Church.

One of the many casualties of the blitz, this was destroyed by incendiaries in 1941. Now only the entrance steps can be seen, the site itself being occupied by a private car park and garages.
A church was built in Cambridge Road about 1890 and this became the Sunday School and Hall when a more elaborate building was erected alongside in 1905 approximately. This was a large structure with galleries on three sides and an organ. It would appear that music was important as in the early part of the century the organist is noted as Mr. Parkinson and the choirmaster a Mr. Chesterfield. It was said to be very well attended with congregation normally about 500 at a Sunday service. On special occasions a former worshipper here says that so crowded was the building that extra chairs were sometimes put in the aisles and there were people actually sitting in the pulpit!
The main church is gone but buildings still exist by the side and these appear to be unused at present. A tablet on one reads: 'Ford Wesleyan Sunday School' and in the apex of the roof of the same wall: 'Hither hath the Lord helped us. Laid by D. Harvey, Esq.' On another adjoining building: 'Ebenezer Wesleyan Sunday School, Rebuilt 1923'.

As has been noted, the church was never re-erected but the war damage compensation enabled a new Methodist church to be built in Halcyon Road to replace the older structure there which is now used as a Hall.

Ford Methodist is no more but it still lives in the memories of some older people.

Greenbank Methodist Church.

This was built in 1886 at a cost of £13,000. It is a daughter church of Zion whose members contributed nearly £1,000 towards its erection.

The first entry in the Baptismal register is dated 12th January 1887 and reads: 'Richard Oscar Hooper, son of Oscar Hooper, Carpenter'. Later on we have: 'Walter Percival, son of F.C. Turner, sailor of 30, Baring Street on 2nd February, 1887'. The Minister at this time was Rev. Alex. Trengrove.

The accounts book (established 1887) is also of interest, first entry being: 'Received from Mrs. Stapleton …. 5s 8½d.' and on 20th February, 1893 we find: 'Cream sold …. 1s.' It is assumed this must have been in connection with a party or other social function. An early account describes the building as of stone, in the Romanesque style and with 620 sittings. The organ was opened in 1890, the contractor being a Mr. Tucker.

This was a fine large church with galleries on three sides with the large organ fitted behind the platform. There were many rooms for church and other purposes attached to the building and the Matthew Hall was added to the south side in 1953.

The structure was badly damaged in the blitz and subsequently repaired.

For some time before its closure in 1976, some of the rooms had been let for industrial purposes (hospital sewing and general repairs) and now in 1977 the building stands empty, and the future is not known.

An excellent church with some stained glass of note, one window shows the Lord and is headed:-
'I AM THE WAY   THE TRUTH   AND THE LIFE' and this particular window commemorates the founding of the first Bible Christian Society in Lake Farm House, Shebbear, Devon, on Monday evening, 9th October 1815.
It is sad to think that such a good church should pass into disuse.
Note: Rugged cross made from wood of this church now incorporated in renovated Tamerton Church.

Ker Street Wesleyan Methodist Chapel, Devonport.

This no longer exists and at present the site is occupied by a block of flats. Incorporated in the wall of the present building is the original stone from the church, which simply states:-
'KER STREET CHAPEL, 1785'. A later tablet notes:-
'……1746, JOHN WESLEY PREACHED HERE AND PLYMOUTH METHODISM WAS BORN…..CHAPEL BUILT 1766. BUILDING DEMOLISHED IN 1961 TO MAKE WAY FOR MODERN FLATS'.
From the above we see a certain confusion of dates and the likely explanation of this is that John Wesley preached on the site (he often spoke in the open air) in 1746 and twenty years later the permanent chapel was built. Probably the stone dated 1785 refers to an alteration or perhaps extension to the premises.
The Ker Street Church is remembered as a square and very plain structure behind Devonport Guildhall. This part of Devonport has undergone so much reconstruction that it is hard to visualise the former buildings.
In the early part of the 19th century before construction of the Column, Mount Zion Chapel, Guildhall and Egyptian Hall (all by Foulston) this part was known as Windmill Hill and was the site of a bowling green.

King Street Methodist Church.

In the year 1864, a small farm house in Flora Street was used for religious meetings. Later in the same year the foundation stone was laid for a permanent church and although no school was included in the original plans, ground had been secured to enable this to be added later.

A church to seat 1,600 was erected in 1866 on the Barley House Estate and a school opened in 1871. The building used to face on King Street and the school at the side was in Tracey Street. It is difficult to pinpoint the exact location but the church would have been sited on what is now the lower part of the market and Frankfort Gate.

Extension took place in 1894 and on this occasion the stone laying ceremony was marred by the collapse of scaffolding (temporary platform) killing one person and injuring 41 others.

Additions were also made in 1907 to provide premises for The Boys Brigade.

This fine church was destroyed in the 1941 blitz, services then being transferred to school premises and later to Nissen huts.

After the war it was hoped to rebuild on the same site but City planning prevented this as the site was needed for a new market. An alternative site adjoining the Crescent was selected and a new church with spacious additional rooms, hall and caretaker's residence opened in 1957 (the stone was laid 18/7/56 by Mr. Lawrence Spear).

The church itself and the main hall are remarkably lofty and it is thought that this was done intentionally to match Foulston's work in the Crescent of which the new premises now form part.

This excellent red brick building and site cost in excess of £133,000 and still keeps the original name of 'King Street Methodist'. A modern but graceful group which fits in well with its surroundings.

Mutley Methodist Church.

In 1867, when Mutley was almost a rural district, Methodist services were commenced in a converted carpenter's shed (cost of conversion was £50) which stood on the site of the present Hyde Park School. A Sunday School was also opened in the kitchen of a nearby farm.

The new church was opened in 1881, the cost of erection being £7,000. When originally built it was in the Plympton area as the dividing line between Plymouth and Plympton at that time ran down though the centre of Mutley Plain. The structure was sited on a former hayfield owned by Jacob Moses of Meavy. An early photograph of the church shows one of Billy Baskerville's horse buses outside, on its way back from Roborough.

The building has been described as 'of limestone with Portland stone dressings. In the Gothic style. Has a tower in the south west angle. Nearly 1,000 sittings and basement school rooms for 400'. A fine stained glass window (now removed) formed the main light on the western side over the main entrance, a tablet below it stating: 'The above window was presented to the trustees of this chapel by W. Derry, Esq. Mayor of Plymouth 1880'. He was, of course, the Derry associated with Derry's clock, this sometimes being known to old Plymothians as 'the four faced deceiver'.

This large, well proportioned church had a spire formerly surmounted by a weathercock, but when this became rusty, and possibly dangerous, it was taken down and replaced by a cross.

Due perhaps in part to changes in population density in the district, to the regret of many, this fine old building was closed early in 1977.

The last Minister to serve was the Rev. Thomas S. Nicholas.

Note: Communion table and lectern now installed at Tamerton Methodist Church.

Pennycross Methodist Church.

It is odd to start notes on a church with the Battle of Waterloo, yet there is some connection.

Napoleon, defeated at the battle in 1815, was held in the Bellerophon which was anchored in the Sound. It was at Belair House that Lord Keith, Sir H. Banbury and Admiral Sir Thomas Duckworth met in the dining room and the final papers were signed relating to the exile of Napoleon to St. Helena. Belair House at that time was a fine building (a contemporary photo does exist) and the seat of Capt. Elphinstone. It was in Montpelier Road on a site now occupied by the higher part of Elphinstone Road, the Plymouth Directory of 1812 describing it as 'a very neat cottage with pretty gardens….'

It was in the same dining room of Belair House that services were commenced in 1899. Mr. R.A.J. Walling, whose excellent book 'The Story of Plymouth' is well known, wrote at the time: 'I saw the dining room of Belair House filled with the youth of Pennycross …. whilst the constable's ducks and chickens enjoyed the sunshine of the remains of the lawn'. The constable referred to was the caretaker as well as having his official duties. Thus started Pennycross Methodist Church.

The congregation grew and for a time meetings were held at Montpelier School. The need for more suitable premises became apparent and a site was purchased at the eastern end of Forest Avenue.

At this time, the old church hall of St. Barnabas in Wilton Street was being replaced by a stone structure so this old hall, a composite building of wood and iron was bought and re-erected at Forest Avenue, the work being carried out by Messrs. Pearn Bros.

This church, or 'Tin Tabernacle' as it was sometimes called, was opened in 1907 and was able to accommodate 250 persons. Belair House was demolished about 1908 and the name 'Belair' and that of Capt. Elphinstone are commemorated in the present roads which must have been built in part on the grounds of this 'neat cottage'.

The population of the district grew and further expansion became necessary. It was proposed to build a more permanent church. The location of the old 'Tin Tab' was not considered suitable so a site was purchased directly opposite in Beauchamp Road for £850. Later a fine new limestone building was erected (said to be in the Gothic style), the foundation stone having been laid by the Mayor of Devonport, Alderman E. Blackall, J.P. in 1913. The church was opened for worship on 25th February, 1914, those being present at the ceremony being Mr. Isaac Foot and Mr. and Mrs. Henry Hurrell. The old wooden hut which had given so much good service was then moved and added to the rear of the new stone building (the site of the old 'Tin Tab' has now been built on although the granite capped limestone pillars which formed the entrance can still be seen in Beauchamp Road). Later various additions and improvements were made to the church and a new organ fitted in 1929 to replace the old American organ previously used.

During the war years the church escaped serious damage but in the post war years a new building became desirable. The St. Levan Church in Stuart Road had been destroyed and the war damage compensation was 'ported' to permit the erection of a completely new church adjoining the old in Beachamp Road.

This new building was opened in 1959 and incorporated in the outer wall is a stone from St. Levan which reads:

STONE LAID BY E. ST. AUBYN, J.P, DECEMBER 8th 1897.

Inside the lobby is a plaque:

'THIS CHURCH OPENED ON OCTOBER 21st, 1959 BY MR. E.L. RICHARDS AND DEDICATED BY REV. RUSSELL. J. POPE. THE TRUSTEES OF ST. LEVAN METHODIST CHURCH WHICH WAS DESTROYED BY ENEMY ACTION IN 1942 DECIDED NOT TO REBUILD AND GENEROUSLY AGREED THAT THE COMPENSATION PAID SHOULD BE

USED TO ERECT THIS CHURCH AND NEW SCHOOLROOMS'.

On the opening of the new building, the old ex St. Barnabas hall was demolished and the former stone church adjoining became and still is a church hall for social activities and Sunday School. It is now known as Wesley Hall.

Additions were made in 1958 and rooms named 'St. Levan Room' and 'Belair Room' perpetuate these particular associations.

In 1956 the pipe organ had been sold and a new electronic two manual instrument obtained and this was subsequently transferred to the 1959 church.

The present Pennycross Methodist Church is a lofty red brick structure, fairly plain outside, modern and fresh inside.

Apart from regular religious services and functions, many social activities take place. Much good work is also carried out to assist various charities by the regular monthly newspaper collections.

An active church, one to which we are invited to 'COME AS A FAMILY' to quote from the notice board.

Whitleigh Methodist Church.

When Whitleigh Estate was being built, a need for a Methodist meeting place existed. At first services were held in a canteen used by the men working on the new housing and later transferred to an old barn. This barn was converted to serve as a church and hall and was in use until the opening of the new permanent Church in 1961. The new building was financed by the Trustees of the Ebrington Street Methodist Church and it cost £40,000. On 20th June, 1959 a service was conducted by the Rev. S. Quick of Peverell Park and this was followed by a public tea at St. Chad's Hall, Whitleigh Green.

The laying of the foundation stone was performed by the Rev. Clifford Lever and this was followed by a Thanksgiving service. The new Church had been launched. It was complete and dedicated

by the Rev. Leonard Tudor on 21st January, 1961, the opening ceremony being performed by Albert Radcliffe, Esq.
Representatives of Anglian, Baptist and Congregational churches took part in the service which was attended by 600 persons. In fact, this event was so well attended that the proceedings were relayed to a further 250 people who were accommodated in the adjoining Sunday School.
The font was dedicated by the Rev. Maurice Harker of King Street, the pulpit by the Rev. Clifford Lever and the communion table by the Rev. Arthur Revell.
At present from the outside one sees a modern red brick building with a hall attached. The church has a small spire and despite its functional appearance it fits in well in this recently built estate and is greatly enhanced by its setting of trees.
Note: Plaque on single manual organ: 'This is to record the gratitude of the congregation of Whitleigh Methodist Church. For the organ received as a gift from the Garrison of St. Alban, Plumer Barracks, Crownhill, after closure of that church on September 12th, 1971.'

Stonehouse Methodist Mission, formerly Stonehouse Wesleyan Methodist Church.

This is one of the original Wesleyan Churches in Plymouth, the first being that in Ker Street, Devonport, built in 1785.
Stonehouse Church was opened in 1813 and was one of the Garrison Churches for the Royal Marines whose barracks was, and still is, in nearby Durnford Street. To commemorate this connection with the Services, the Royal Crest appears on the balustrade of the gallery.
The building was altered in 1857 and a Sunday School block added in 1884.
Until the 1960's the internal arrangements resembled those of Mutley and Greenbank Methodist churches, but about 1961 a floor was inserted above the lower part of the building which then

provided a hall in the upper part. This makes the ceiling of the church proper rather low but certainly makes efficient use of the space available.

Since it was built in 1813 the district has seen many changes, factories and business premises being erected in the place of dwellings in what was once a well populated area.

In 1977 the Mission continues to serve and is ably run by Pastor Robert Stivey. It provides a community meeting place as well as one for religious observances, and has many social activities.

Crownhill Methodist Church.

In 1812 a Methodist Chapel at Knacker's Hole in the parish of St. Budeaux was registered for public worship. We know little of this - it may have been a separate building or possibly just a room in a private house. Shortly afterwards, we hear of a Sunday School being formed by a Mr. John Ellis who was Superintendent for 40 years and played a large part in the life of Wesleyan society in the area.

Associated with Ebenezer Chapel in Saltash Street was a Richard Lethbridge, a baker and grocer of Old Town Street. In 1817 he built a chapel on a site which was later occupied by Davis's Garage. The chapel was said to have accommodated eighty persons sitting and thirty standing. Parts of the walls and windows can still be seen inside the garage.

The names of the first trustees make interesting reading: Thomas Tanner, baker, John Williams, printer and bookbinder, John Clarkson, grocer. Daniel Shepheard, chymist, William Vyvyan, carver and turner, Phillip Shepheard, saddler, Samuel Davis, purser R.N., John Murch, painter, John Ellis, gardener and James Neal, farmer. Mostly middle class tradesmen and all men of good will. The chapel was sold to the Government in 1863 for £500 (H.M. Government had certain defence plans which included clearing that part of houses but like so many official schemes, this was never done). This £500 was lent to the trustees of the new Wesleyan Chapel erected in King Street in 1866.

But back to Crownhill. For some time the Crownhill Chapel continued to be used, being rented from the Government but in 1870 the ground on which the present church stands was bought for £150 and the memorial stone for the new church was laid on 3rd May, 1871. The ceremony ended with the singing of the National Anthem. Later the same day a service was conducted by the Rev. Charles Wilson of Sherwell.

The new chapel was opened on 5th July, 1871. It was built of limestone with Bath stone dressing and had 168 seats. A Sunday School was erected in 1888.

The church was originally lighted by oil but gas was installed in 1904 and electricity in 1920. Due to overcrowding it was decided to extend the building and when this had been done it was opened by the Mayoress, Mrs. J.F. Winnicott in February, 1907.

In 1927 the church was redecorated and in 1950 the platform and new organ were dedicated.

The Herbert Street Chapel had been destroyed during the war and in 1959 it was decided to 'port' about 513,000 war damage payment to enable the new Sunday school to be built. Now in 1977, further alterations and improvements have been made.

Crownhill Methodist Church has seen many changes in the district. Originally near a busy cross road junction, at the corner of which was a blacksmith's shop (Spry's Forge), now fronting on a modern traffic complex. But the aim of service to God and the maintenance of moral standards remains the same.

St. Levan Methodist Church, Stuart Road.

Said to have been opened in 1888, it was destroyed in 1941. It was decided not to rebuild.

The war damage compensation was used to erect a new church and schoolrooms to replace the old building at Beauchamp Road. A

stone from the St. Levan Church is embodied in the new Pennycross Methodist Church and reads:
'STONE LAID BY E. ST.AUBYN, J.P. DECEMBER 8th, 1897'. It is assumed that this is a memorial stone, possibly relating to some extension of the St. Levan Church, or perhaps the building destroyed in the war superseded an earlier, smaller place of worship.

St. Budeaux Methodist Church, Victoria Road.

In 1880, Methodists of the area first met in disused stables, and later in cottages in Victoria Road.
A move was made to Vicarage Road (now re-named Normandy Way) in 1892. A school hall was erected in Stirling Road in 1938 and was named the Gloucester Hall.
During the last war, the Methodist Church at Gloucester Street, Morice Town, was destroyed and the war damage compensation provided resources to enable a fine new red brick building to be erected in Victoria Road in 1956. Besides the church itself, public rooms for social and other activities are attached.

Peverell Methodist Church.

Situated at the Plymouth end of Peverell Park Road, it was started in 1891 by members of the Mutley Church. Initially services had been held in the open air and later in two rooms of a cottage.
An iron building was erected in 1896 and this was supplanted by the present church opened in 1905. There are many stones in the foundation, one reads: 'H.J. Hurrell, J.P. Mayor. May 4th, 1904'. Subsequently the church was enlarged and classrooms added. (Stone: Sunday School. 1928).
The original iron building survived until 1965 when it was demolished to make way for a car park. At this time, too, ground in excess of the needs of the church was sold for the building of private dwelling houses.

A fine limestone building catering in part for the now closed churches of Greenbank and Mutley.

Wesleyan Methodist Chapel, Ebrington Street.

The early history appears a bit complicated but it seems that in 1831 a large hall had been erected by the Plymouth Brethren (see separate details). This was a squarish, angular, structure sometimes referred to as 'the Dutch Oven', and seated 1,000 persons. It was sold to the Methodists in 1857.
The premises were re-built to seat 650 in 1897 (Architect: H.J. Snell).
In 1936, the widening of Cobourg Street took place and this necessitated the demolition of the Primitive Methodist Church which had existed at the junction of Cobourg and York Streets and in 1937 the Cobourg Memorial Hall was built adjoining the Ebrington Street Chapel to provide extra accommodation for members of the Primitive Methodist Church who had joined.
It was in 1937 that the premises at Ebrington Street were gutted by fire and the congregation rendered homeless. They then joined the Ebenezer Church in Saltash Street and the merged congregations became part of what in 1940 was renamed the Plymouth Methodist Central Hall. The gutted chapel in Ebrington Street was partly restored and was used for many years as Sellecks's Restaurant. Completely demolished in the late 1960's, the site was used for premises for a builders' merchant and is now occupied by MFI Industries.

Keyham Methodist Church.

For the origin of this church we go back to 1887 when meetings were held at the home of a Mrs. Foxwell at 28, Johnston Terrace, Keyham.
In due course, an iron building 'the Tin Tabernacle' was erected in Admiralty Street. The influence of this new church spread and soon

the Admiralty wanted to hold parade services there. The iron building became too small for the increased congregation and a new home for the church was found in Johnston Terrace Board School.

It was decided that a large, permanent church was necessary and a site was given by Lord St. Levan. The foundation stone was laid in 1901 and the building opened by Mrs. W.J. Moon in October 1902. Queen Victoria had died in the same year as the foundation stone had been laid and the new church was called 'Keyham Victoria'. The church had been built to accommodate 1,000 persons with Sunday School seating for 600 children. Extensions were made in 1925.

During the 1939/45 war great use was made of the building as a rest centre and to help many bombed out families during this difficult period.

Very recently extensive alterations and modernisation of the internal arrangements have been carried out, and it is interesting to note that the organ which was built and dedicated by the organist, Mr. T. Hele, is now being re-installed at the Church of St. James the Less, Ham.

Keyham Methodist is a fine church which has seen many changes but has adapted well to modern times.

Cobourg Street Primitive Methodist Church.

This was a fair sized building situated at the top of York Street junction with Cobourg Street on a site which is now occupied by the North Cross underpass, just outside the YMCA.

When Cobourg Street was widened in 1936, the premises were demolished and the congregation joined those of the Wesleyan Methodist Chapel in Ebrington Street.

The church was an imposing building with a battlemented appearance and having a small four sided spire. It occupied the corner site, had iron railings and was approached by shallow steps.

Methodist Chapel in Gloucester Street, Morice Town.

Said to have been built in 1811, it was destroyed in the blitz of 1941. It was never re-erected and the site is now occupied by school premises.
The war damage compensation was 'ported' to enable a fine new church to be built in Victoria Road, St. Budeaux.

Albert Road Methodist Church.

This stood at the lower end of Albert Road just below where the Royal Sailors Rest exists. It was at the junction of Albert Road and Charlotte Street. Previously known as the Salem Chapel.

Mount Gould Methodist Church.

This was started in a barn in 1904 but later in that year a church was built and opened. This is a large limestone building and seats 500 persons. It has a Sunday School attached.
An addition, known as the Jinkin Institute, was built in 1935 at a cost of £2,700.

Mill Bridge Methodist Church.

Built in 1897 beside what is now Victoria Park. At the time of building, Mill Bridge actually had a tide mill and the water extended up to and beyond Pennycomequick.
A memorial stone - perhaps relating to some extension - notes: 'Laid by John Bright James, Esq. Mayor of Devonport, July 3rd, 1895'.
Close to the former Mill Bridge toll gate, freed in 1924.

St. George's Road Methodist Church.

Situated at the junction of St. George's Road and Ryder Road, this was built in 1898 and destroyed in the blitz of 1941.
A school hall was erected in 1954 and the church rebuilt at a cost of £30,000 in 1964.
Little of the original church can be seen, only the entrance steps and boundary walls remaining from the former building.

Belmont Methodist Church, Stoke.

Described in the Plymouth Directory for 1899 as 'an excellent Gothic building', this large church faces the top of Albert Road, Devonport, and adjoins the grounds of Belmont House (one of Foulston's masterpieces).
The church was opened in 1876 and seats 500. In the basement of the building is a school hall.

Embankment Road Methodist Church.

This was built in 1898 and is a daughter church of Greenbank. It is assumed that the district was growing, thereby necessitating a new church.
It is a large limestone building at the junction of Embankment Road and Cattedown Road. It overlooks a busy traffic roundabout (formerly crossroads complete with horse trough) and must have seen many changes. Has 750 sittings.

Tamerton Methodist Church.

The original church at Tamerton is said to have seated 80 persons. It was sited a little up the road from the present church on or about the garden of a house now known as 'the White Cottage'. The document of title to part of this property dated 1813 refers to the "Chapel or Meeting House now and for several years past used and appropriated for religious purposes by the Society of Protestant

Dissenters denominated Methodist, in connection with the late Mr. John Wesley, situated in Tamerton Church Town within the parish of Tamerton Foliot".

The present church was opened on 6th June, 1877 and the interior has recently (1977) been redesigned. During the last two years voluntary workers have completely redecorated the building and removed the pulpit as this was felt to be too remote from the congregation.

The sanctuary has been altered, partly by the addition of a beautiful carved Communion Table and Lectern which came from the now closed Mutley Methodist Church (1867 - 1881 - 1977). Also incorporated during the recent alterations is a large plain cross made from wood from the now closed Greenbank Church (1886 - 1976).

These changes have made the church very attractive and have created a feeling of spaciousness.

Note: A later deed dated March 1865 relates to the sale to the Chapel Trustees of an additional piece of land and building, used as a schoolroom connected with the Wesleyan Methodists Chapel.

An excellent booklet recently published by the Tamerton Village Conservation Society notes that Wesleyan Methodism had been a factor of village life since 1800 (about). At first there was no regular Minister although it is recorded that he was required to preach only 'the doctrines that are contained in the notes and sermons of the Rev. John Wesley …. and no other doctrines …. and perform other acts of religious worship in conformity with the said doctrines only and for no other purpose'.

Ernesettle Methodist Church.

This is a modern structure near Ernesettle Green and is near the main shopping area of the district.

It was opened with classrooms and clubrooms in 1958.

Halcyon Road Methodist Church.

This is a daughter church of Greenbank (now closed).
In the 1920's when the Swilly Corporation Housing Estate came into being, a wooden hut in the area served as a Sunday School.
In 1924 a new church was built and although this still stands it was replaced by a more modern structure in 1952.
This stands on ground adjoining the older church and members of the blitzed St. Levan, Morice Square, Gloucester Street and Ford churches, as well as those living locally, are said to have joined the congregation.
The erection of the newer building was financed by the war damage compensation which had been 'ported' from the destroyed Ford Methodist Church in Cambridge Road.
Halcyon Road Church is of modern design and has ancillary rooms for social activities. Together with the older building (which now serves as a hall) these are undoubtedly a great asset to the neighbourhood.

Zion Methodist Church, The Hoe, Plymouth.

Early in the nineteenth century, a group of Bible Christians were worshipping in an old sail loft near the Barbican. In 1842 a church to accommodate 550 persons was built in Zion Street off Citadel Road. Beneath the church itself was a schoolroom to hold 300.
A contemporary photo shows it to have had quite an elaborate frontage, the main entrance on Zion Street being approached by two short flights of steps. Internally, it had extensive galleries with an ornate arch forming the front of the organ space. The organ seems to be quite a large one. Much work must have gone into the furnishings of this attractive building.
Zion was noted for its warmth and vigour and was regrettably destroyed in the 1941 blitz after serving the district well for nearly 100 years.

Laira Methodist Church, now renamed Zion Methodists.

An excellent booklet published at the opening of Zion in 1957 notes the following: 'Methodism had its inception in Laira in 1892 when services were held in a room in Elm Terrace, the Avenue.
In 1897 this room was acquired by the Great Western Railway, and the church had to seek other premises.
After wandering here and there, Laira Green Primary School, the YMCA in Old Laira Road, the church was opened on its present site by the Mayor of Devonport (W.J. Moon, Esq) on 21st March, 1906'.
The booklet goes on to say that the cost of the land was £460 and the building was erected by Messrs. Pearn Bros. at a price of £1,413. The debt on the premises was cleared by 1922 and an organ installed in 1938. The Jubilee of Methodism in Laira was celebrated in 1942.
As has been noted previously, the Zion Church near the Hoe had been destroyed by enemy action in 1941. The war damage compensation was 'ported' to Laira and enabled a completely new church to be constructed on land adjoining the old building and the opening in 1957 is commemorated by two tablets which read: 'To the Glory of God, this church was built in place of Zion Methodist Church, Plymouth, destroyed by enemy action 21st March, 1941'. And the other. 'To the Glory of God this stone was laid by the Rt. Hon. Isaac Foot, P.C, 21st May, 1956'. These two stones appear on either side of the main entrance in Wycliffe Road.
Contractors for the new building were Messrs. Godolphin Co. Ltd. And the architect Mr. V.C.L. Saunders, ARIBA.
The interior is light and pleasant. The two outstanding features are the illuminated cross at the front of the building and the Zion memorial window at the rear over the main entrance. It expresses the Biblical theme Zion, the Community of God. It was unveiled and dedicated on 14th September, 1961, and its coloured glass forms an attractive characteristic.

The new premises also contain rooms for social and other activities and must add much to the religious and communal life of the district.

The old (1906) church is now used as a hall, part of the time serving to house a Playgroup.

Finally, to quote again from the 1957 booklet: 'The history .... is a story of labour freely and lovingly given' and there is little doubt that this comment is justified.

Other chapels and meeting places are said to have existed at:

Salem Chapel, Salem Street, Plymouth.

Millbrook Cottage, St. Budeaux.

Market Street, Stonehouse.

Edgcumbe Street, Stonehouse.

Granby Ope, Devonport.

Mount Street, Devonport.

Camden Street, Plymouth.

College Road, Keyham.

Bridwell Road, St. Budeaux.

Barton Avenue, Keyham.

ROMAN CATHOLIC

Church of Christ the King, The Hoe, Plymouth.

Situated on what was formerly the south west corner of Princess Square, this very attractive church stands at the Hoe end of what is now Armada Way.

Built in 1962 as a chapel-of-ease to the Cathedral, it was designed by Sir Gilbert Scott who was notable because of his connection with the building of Liverpool's Anglican Cathedral.

It is a brick building of unusual but pleasing design. Internally it is a lofty structure with slender pillars, and has a small gallery at the rear. The main entrance is on the northern side and faces Royal

Parade. Over the door is a carving of a lamb with a Latin inscription: 'Adveniat Regnum Tuum' – 'Thy Kingdom Come'. About 1970 the building exhibited certain constructional troubles but these have now been overcome. The church stands out amid the box like formation of our modern shops and nearby hotel and the route to the Hoe is enhanced by its presence.

Church of the Holy Redeemer, Keyham.

The foundation stone for this building was laid in 1901 the first Mass to be said there was in 1902.
The church was damaged during the 1941 blitz when services were held for a time in the adjoining school.
Subsequently the Church of the Holy Redeemer was restored and reopened, being blessed by Bishop Grimshaw in 1950.

The Church of the Holy Family, Beacon Park.

Great strides were made in housing in the Swilly and Beacon Park area during the 1920/1930 period and the need for a Catholic place of worship in the district became manifest.
Before the last war, the need was met by use being made by the public of a small wooden chapel of the Ursuline Nuns, a teaching Order using the premises formerly known as 'Prospect'. The Sisters left in 1931 and the buildings were taken over by St. Boniface College, which had up to that time been located in Wyndham Square. The wooden chapel which had been used by courtesy of the Nuns continued to provide facilities for the public by permission of the College Authorities until 1941 when it was destroyed by enemy action. St. Boniface then permitted the use of the hall within the main building.
Before the war the need for a proper church had been recognised and to this end money had been subscribed and plans drawn up. After the war the matter became urgent and a church was built in 1955 on a plot of ground adjoining the school. Owing to building

and other controls at that time (many will recall the shortage of materials and labour during that era) the original plans were not followed and the new church was of rather a utility nature to start with. The altar was a makeshift and was actually supported on two oil drums. Later, however, a new marble altar - a copy of the one at Lourdes in France - was installed and internal arrangements greatly improved under the guidance of the noted architect, Louis de Soissons.

Subsequently a presbytery and church hall were added and the church now has two resident priests.

Note: Brass crucifix on high altar a gift from Mr Hutty. Statue on lady altar was by an Irish sculptor and given by Mrs. Chapman.

Holy Cross Church.

This church is sited very close to the old LSWR rail terminal (Friary Station) and seems to have a definite railway connection. It would appear that the Church of St. Charles in Teignmouth (built 1843) was constructed very near the railway line, and when in 1884 East Cliff tunnel was opened out (possibly to accommodate the new Teignmouth Station) it became necessary to demolish the church. The stone from this building was brought to Plymouth (an easy task owing to the proximity of both rail lines) and Holy Cross erected. Thus we have a Teignmouth church transferred to Plymouth.

Alterations and/or additions have been made in 1876, 1900, 1914 and 1920 and work to improve the building is still going on.

The original church was much smaller than the present and consists mainly of the rear three quarters - the division between the old and the later can clearly be seen. Two interesting stone tablets exist at the back of the church let into the wall but the history of these is not known.

The architect for the church was Hansom (who also designed the Cathedral) and it is said to be in the Gothic style with 600 sittings. Although there is little doubt about the origin of the church, the dates given and the exact tunnel which was opened are not certain, dates of 1874 and 1882 have also been given as those of the original erection of Holy Cross Church.

Our Lady of Mount Carmel, Efford.

A Carmelite Convent was built at Efford about 1920, the building being situated in extensive grounds (formerly Efford House, home of the Clarke family). At that time the chapel could be used by the public but because the Carmelites are an enclosed order, they were separated and out of sight of the main body of the church by an iron grille.
In 1954, due to housing growth in the area, the Convent became surrounded by buildings and the Nuns left. The Chapel then became the Church of our Lady of Mount Carmel.
A parish was created in 1957 and the premises modified in 1964. Further alterations were carried out in 1975, notably the removal of the altar from the east wall to a more central position. The iron grille mentioned above has been removed although its former position is still visible.
It is believed that certain building is likely to take place soon in the extensive grounds.

Church of St. Edward the Confessor, Holland Road, Peverell.

Started in 1911 and completed in 1933, this church is said to be in the Romanesque style and has 250 sittings.
During the post war period certain internal changes have taken place. The original marble altar has been replaced by one in granite and moved to another position. The marble altar rails have also been changed, the present ones being made of granite.
The building also has a marble pulpit and more recently a fine statue of St. Edward had been added.
An excellent church hall has been built since the war on a site opposite the church building.

The Cathedral of St. Mary and St. Boniface, Wyndham Street, Plymouth.

The first registers date from 1792 when a chapel was formed in a room over the George Inn, Devonport (then known as 'Dock'). This was used until the early years of the nineteenth century when a chapel was erected in Stonehouse in 1806 and dedicated in 1807 to St. Mary and St. John. The street became known as St. Mary's Street and until recent years there existed a small statue in a niche on the front wall of one of the houses. Much reconstruction has taken place in this district but it would be interesting to know what happened to this figure.

The Cathedral in Wyndham Street was founded by Bishop Vaughan who bought the present site for one shilling and three pence (about 6p today) per square foot. The Architects were Joseph and Charles Hansom (Joseph was the designer of the Hansom Cab) and the contractor a Mr. W. Roberts of Stonehouse who undertook to construct the shell of the building and complete the nave for £3,800. Troubles seem to have beset the building in its early stages; when the roof was finished in 1857 and other work was going ahead, cracks appeared in the structure south of the nave. In an effort to save the situation two pillars were shored up but the efforts were in vain as the brickwork fell taking with it the whole of the roof of the nave and the south clerestory. Later, on the eve of the feast of St. Boniface, the chancel fell down. These disasters were said by some to be the result of heavy gunfire in the Sound but it seems likely that there may have been other causes. Troubles did not end there as there was a gas explosion in the Episcopal residence but happily no one was hurt.

The Cathedral was opened in March 1858. Later a spire, 205 feet high was added in 1867 and an organ installed - a noteworthy point on this instrument was that it came from St. Martins in the Fields, London, and had been played by Handel.

An early description notes: '.... a cruciform building in the Early English Style opened in 1858 but not consecrated until 1880.

Consists of choir with aisles, transepts with eastern chapels, nave, aisles and a tower with spire 205 feet high erected in 1866 containing one bell. Sacristy forms part of a separate building and leads to the Bishop's residence .... carved stone reredos erected in 1899 .... in 1921 the Lady Chapel was transformed and a diocesan memorial to those from the Plymouth Diocese who fell in the Great War 1914-1918 erected, and at the same time the organ was placed in the chapel originally designed for it, while a new altar to the Sacred Heart was erected in the transept. There are 750 sittings'. The organ previously mentioned has been reconstructed on several occasions. The Chapel of the Blessed Sacrament has an alabaster altar and a wrought iron screen. The Lady Chapel has four stone figures representing King David, Saints Joachim and Anne, and John the Evangelist. Supporting the statue of the Blessed Virgin is a reredos depicting Mary sorrowing, and Mary being crowned Queen of Heaven.

Bishop Vaughan died in 1902 and in 1904 a memorial window with a tablet beneath was erected in his memory.

Adjoining the Cathedral was the Convent of Notre Dame. This Order acquired the remaining building in the block, that of the former Presbyterian Church, mainly for use as a school hall, in 1936.

During the last war the Convent premises were badly damaged and the old Presbyterian building was almost completely destroyed. The Convent and school moved to Derriford after the war and at present the old premises are used for Further Education.

The remains of the former Presbyterian Church were used during the war period as a static water tank and then remained derelict until September 1977 when they were demolished.

So many changes have taken place and due to post war reconstruction of the City and expansion, the Cathedral which was once centrally located no longer is so. Other Catholic churches have been built to meet the needs of a spreading City, notably the fine Church of St. Peter at Crownhill.

Church of St. Michael and Joseph, James Street, Devonport.

At the end of the eighteenth century there was a chapel in a room over a stable at the rear of the George Inn, Devonport. In 1806 a chapel was erected in St. Mary Street, Stonehouse.
Until 1859 Bishop Vaughan had been unable to secure a site for a permanent church in Devonport but this difficulty was finally overcome and a stone laid for the new building in 1860. The contractor was Mr. W. Roberts and the architect Joseph Hansom, both of whom had been associated with the new Cathedral in Plymouth.
The solemn opening took place in 1861 and the church completed by the addition of the sanctuary and the north aisle with the Lady Chapel at a later date. This work was carried out by Messrs. Palk and Partridge to the design of a London architect, Herbert Gribble. Mr. Gribble was born in Plymouth and was also responsible for the Armada monument on the Hoe.
James Street and the Mutton Cove area were once busy spots but in recent years many people have moved away and the thriving little community at Mutton Cove no longer exists.
St. Michael and Joseph's was one of Devonport's Garrison churches attended by members of both the Navy and the Army - parties sometimes paraded to the church headed by bands.
Still of note are the stained glass windows over the High altar. These are of St. Joseph, St. Michael, St. George and St. Patrick. Formerly a school was attached but this has moved and is now situated near the St. Aubyn Church on ground that previously was part of Raglan Barracks. The new school has a small but attractive chapel.

The Church of St. Paul, St. Budeaux.

This is an unusual square building in Pemross Road and was built in 1933 by funds provided by the two Miss Robinsons, who also gave financial aid to enable churches to be built at Crownhill,

Exeter and Torquay.

Modelled on the Church of St. Paul in Rome, some internal alterations have been made since it was originally constructed, one of these changes being the removal of the dome over the High Altar.

The front of the church which faces Pemross Road is rather striking. Over the main entrance is a circular centrepiece from the centre of which radiates the attributes of God.

Once in a pleasant backwater off St. Budeaux Square, is now on one of the main roads to Cornwall due to the building of the Tamar Road Bridge between 1959 to 1962.

A presbytery, also provided by the generosity of the Miss Robinsons, adjoins the church, which with its surrounding trees and bushes, is a pleasant feature in the district.

Church of St. Peter, Crownhill.

This is the second church of St. Peter to be built in the Crownhill area. From about 1937 onwards a church existed in the Crownhill Road which had been erected by the generosity of the two Miss Robinsons who also provided funds for the provision of churches at St. Budeaux, Exeter and Torquay.

The need for a new church with greater accommodation existed and to this end a foundation stone was laid by the Right Rev. Cyril Restieaux on 2nd August 1969. When the new building was complete the old premises in Crownhill Road became a social club. The present church of St. Peter, which with its adjoining Bishop Vaughan Secondary Modern School, stands not far from the centre of old Crownhill Village. The church itself is outstanding in conception, being circular in form with a glass dome at the apex of the roof.

Internally, the arrangements are such that the altar which serves the main body of the church can also be used to serve a smaller chapel which is at the back of the building. Although the church is unusual in appearance, it is refreshing to see a design that breaks new ground and is not conventional, yet fulfils the present need in such an admirable manner.

Church of St. Thomas More, Bamfylde Way, Southway.

A modern brick fronted structure built in 1964. It serves the needs of a growing district and is architecturally in keeping with its surroundings. A Presbytery is attached.
The interior of the church is light and airy. It has one unusual feature which takes the form of a glass partition to separate one portion of the church where parents may take their children. This ensures that a crying child will not inconvenience others attending the service and is certainly a thoughtful and practical characteristic.

UNITED REFORMED

Derriford United Reformed Church.

This is said to have been started by a member of Mutley Baptist Church named Percival White.
In 1895 a site was purchased on the main road at Derriford and on this was erected a wooden building to seat 100. It was called the Down House Mission and was put on trust "for adults or children only of the working or poorer classes residing in the neighbourhood. The services to be of a helpful character and of Protestant and Evangelical character".
Services were held on Sunday evenings and were usually conducted by local preachers. In 1955 it became Congregational by the wish of those attending.
As the building was becoming inadequate, it was intended to build another larger church on the same site. Owing to proposed road improvements, this could not be done but a site was bought on Powisland Drive nearby.
The foundation stone was laid by the Rev. Frank Quick of Sherwell and reads: TO THE GLORY OF GOD IN THE SERVICE OF MAN, 11th June, 1966.

The cost of the new church which was opened and dedicated in 1966 was partly met by the sale of Emma Place Congregational Church (1787- 1956) in Stonehouse. The new building held about 200.

A community hall was added in 1970 and the Manse in 1974. The organ installed in March 1975 was the gift of Mrs. Tidbury.

The church itself is octagonal and has windows on all sides, making it one of the lightest buildings one is likely to find. It also has white pews and is most attractive. Some alterations have been made to increase the accommodation and it is now thought to seat about 300 persons. Externally, it is seen to have a copper roof and small spire, the surrounding trees and shrubs enhancing its appearance.

Laira United Reformed Church.

Back in 1840 the need existed for a meeting place at the east end of the town. Norley Chapel pioneered work in this area and meetings held at a farm house in Laira were well attended. After a while, a hay loft near the main road at Lower Crabtree was used but this had to be closed and services were then transferred to a room at Marsh Mills.

The next move was to an old coach factory at Higher Crabtree. Larger premises became necessary and a site, on which only two walls stood at first, was rented "at a very reasonable rent" from Mr. G. Soltau. This little Mission flourished and soon became overcrowded.

Sherwell Church was asked to accept affiliation and the foundation stone for a new chapel was laid in 1886 by the then Minister of Sherwell, Rev. C.S. Slater (a stone marked "C.S.S. 1886" is embodied in the present structure). The new building was opened at the end of the same year.

This subsequently became too small and it was intended in 1928 to enlarge the 1886 chapel which had been erected on the south side of the Laira 'narrows'. Corporation plans for road widening prevented this (1977 and the 'narrows' are still there!) and the old site was exchanged in 1934 for another on the north side of the road.

In 1935, a church/hall was built and survived the blitz, it being the only Congregational church in Plymouth to escape damage.

A stone on the building reads: 'Erected to the Glory of God. This stone was laid by Emmanual Rooke, Esq. March 16th, 1935'.

A point of interest here is that the organ installed came from the old Princes Street church Devonport. The Architect for the new structure was F.A. Wiblin, LRIBA and the contractor Messrs. Wakeham Brothers.

The building was extended in 1956/57, the extension being known as the Courtenay Hall, named after the blitzed church which had existed off Union Street, and the present church erected. A plaque in the vestibule notes: "In gratitude to the church sometime gathered in Courtenay Street".

Some of the money for the building of the new (1957) church had come from war damage compensation on the Union Church (1848 - 1941), which had previously existed on a site now taken up by the City Centre.

The Laira Church had been a branch of Sherwell until it became independent in 1937 but close ties still remain.

Pilgrim United Reformed Church, St. Levan Road.

As with Sherwell Church, we cannot do better than start with Andrew Kinsman. Born in Tavistock in 1724, he came to Plymouth in 1743 (see details under Sherwell).

After the commencement of the Tabernacle in Plymouth, he was ordained at Bristol in 1763 and started his work at Dock (Devonport) in the same year. From then until his death in 1793, he was minister for both the Tabernacle and the new meeting place in Devonport, which at first was known as the Lower Room in Queen Street. Later, as numbers grew, another place of worship, the Higher Room, was built in Granby St.

The chapel in Princes St. where the church eventually found its home, was opened in 1801 and after being enlarged several times, it is said to have held 1,200 persons. Thus Devonport had its first Congregational Church. There were certain secessions from Princes St: one settling in South Street and another at Mount Street (this would be the building, remembered no doubt by many older people of Devonport, which existed facing the top of Canterbury St. with the side forming part of the lane between the houses known as 'the Arch' - all traces swept away either during or after the war).
Later, some of the congregation of Mount Street went to Mount Zion Church at the top of Ker Street (site now occupied by Ker Street Infants School), others to the Salem Chapel at the lower end of Albert Road (later to become the Methodist Free Church) and to the Wycliffe Chapel at the top of Albert Road, close to the LSWR Halt. At present the location of Salem would be just below the Royal Sailors Rest and Wycliffe near the garage at the junction of Exmouth Road/Albert Road.
After the First World War, in 1931, the Princes Street premises were sold and the money so realised put towards the erection of a new church in another area. For a time, meetings were held at the Britannia Hall at Milehouse and then a suitable site was found in St. Levan Road where a new church was built and opened in 1934. This was named after George Whitfield (to whom Kinsman had originally owed his conversion. The Wycliffe Chapel was hit by incendiaries and the Whitfield Church in St. Levan Road was destroyed. A remnant of the congregation of Wycliffe continued to worship in a hut at the rear of the burnt out building from 1941 to 1950 and a contemporary photograph shows this Mens Club Hut with the upturned billiards table being used for a platform for the pulpit and communion table. Worship at St. Levan Road continued in a Nissen hut between 1950 to 1953, many members of the congregation having attended Sherwell in the intervening period. In 1949 a decision had been reached to combine the two communities of Whitfield and Wycliffe and in 1950 a new church was formed, taking the name of 'Pilgrim'. The hall/church in St.

Levan road was commenced in 1952 and completed in 1953 with funds from the war damage payments on the destroyed Whitfield Chapel. The new building was used for religious purposes and also used as a hall for other church activities.

In 1958, work on a permanent church in St. Levan Road began. The Nissen hut was demolished - partly by voluntary work of the church members - and in 1959 the new Pilgrim Church was opened and the previous hall/church became the Whitfield Hall, the foundation stone of which now appears in the entrance of Pilgrim. It reads: 'This stone was laid by the Right Worshipful the Mayor of Plymouth, Councillor E. Stanley Leatherby, May 2nd, 1934'

The Architect for Pilgrim was H. Norman Haines, LRIBA, and the contractors, Messrs. F.J. Stanbury Ltd.

Wycliffe has not been forgotten as one of the stones has been laid at the entrance. Noted on the wall above is: "The stone below is part of Wycliffe Congregational Chapel, Albert Road, built 1858, destroyed 1941".

Now this most attractive and modern church (its design makes it appear light and cheerful even on a dull day) with the previous building, the Whitfield Hall and ancillary rooms, a fine compact group exists which serves the district well.

Sherwell United Reformed Church.

We cannot start talking about the history of Sherwell without mentioning Andrew Kinsman (1724 - 1793), born in Tavistock, he came to Plymouth at the age of 19 and set up as a grocer at 6, Breton Side (now Exeter Street). He began to ask a few people to his home to hear him read a sermon and these meetings became so frequent and the attendances so numerous that the room behind the shop which had been used for these religious observances would no longer serve. Kinsman decided to erect a building in the garden behind his house and when this had been done he called it 'TheTabernacle'. It was thus that in 1745 when theTabernacle was opened that Sherwell really began.

In 1750 Kinsman was regarded as the regular minister. This building (later called the 'Old Tabernacle') was said to have seated 400 and the little ope which originally led to the garden and the Tabernacle can still be seen opposite the Salvation Army Hall in Exeter St.

The Tabernacle and congregation had their troubles; on one occasion the building was broken into by a party of seamen led by their lieutenant who intended to put out the lights and "to castigate the congregation". Despite opposition, Kinsman persevered and founded a meeting place (later known as Princes St. Church) at Plymouth Dock about 1750. He was ordained at Bristol in 1763 and was minister of both the Tabernacle and the Princes Street Church until his death in 1793.

His son then took possession of the building and his autocratic behaviour appears to have upset the congregation, who bought land in Norley St. and built the 'New Tabernacle'.

Records of the subsequent use of the Old Tabernacle seem a bit hazy but it appears that it was occupied by the Wesleyan Association (Methodist Free Church) until 1862, and in 1879, 134 years after it had been built, it left the ownership of the Kinsman family. Sherwell Church rented it until 1887 and it was later used by the Mission Band. A member who attended during the early part of this century recalls that it held about 150 persons, was situated in Moon Lane and had a rather plain interior. At the end of the hall was a platform and a table covered with a red velvet cloth, embroidered:- GOD is LOVE in ivy leaves. It was destroyed by enemy action in 1941.

But back to the New Tabernacle in Norley Street. Alterations were made in 1833, during which time services were held at the Mechanics Institute in Princess Square. It was opened again a few months later under the new name of 'Norley Chapel'.

I suppose most religious congregations have their troubles and one is reported that seems somewhat amusing. In 1845 the organ at Norley was in disrepair, so a string band was employed, but "owing to differences of opinion as to who should play the first fiddle, the band did not play". Later a Mrs. Bangham led the singing.

By 1860 the work of the new church had so prospered that despite enlargements and the addition of two galleries, the accommodation became insufficient. Further expansion was impossible owing to surrounding buildings. A new site was sought and one was located just below the reservoir, a site then occupied by a burnt out mill (as a point of interest, Drake's Higher Mill stood nearby). The foundation stone for the new church was laid by Alderman. David Derry and the silver trowel used was for many years in the possession of the Rooker family. A parchment placed under the stone reads: "The Chapel intended to be erected on this site by the Congregational Church founded in the year 1796 and at present worshipping at Norley Chapel, Plymouth, is dedicated to the Glory of God, with fervent prayer for the Divine Blessing, the foundation stone of the building is laid this 4th day of September 1862 by David Derry, Esq." The parchment was signed by Charles Wilson, M.A., Pastor David Derry, Herbert Mends Gibson, Richard Garland, Alfred Rooker, John Plimsaull, Alexander Hubbard, Deacons, and Messr. Paull and Ayscliffe, Architects".

With the parchment, and in a sealed bottle, went three current newspapers and several coins of the realm.

Subsequent efforts to locate this stone have failed, probably because during alterations to the roadway (about 1897 the Dartmoor Inn just on the south side was demolished, the road widened and Queen Anne Terrace built) the surface of the street was raised. Although it is known that the stone is adjacent to the tower, it has never been found; perhaps it will be in the future.

The Church was opened in 1864 and the school premises in 1868. The Norley chapel was then closed, to be opened again later with Sherwell as its Mother Church. Norley was never rebuilt after being destroyed in the 1941 blitz, but the war damage payment enabled a church of the same name to be opened at Plymstock.

As to the name of Sherwell. The new church was built near Sherwell House (the entrance pillars of this can still be seen) but the main reason for the name is to commemorate the Rev. Nicholas Sherwell, M.A. the nonconformist minister who was imprisoned on Drake's Island for 3 months in 1665.

As to the church building. It was the first Gothic nonconformist church to be built in the West Country. The tower, surmounted by the spire, is 135 feet high and at the four corners of the top of the tower are carvings of a man, a lion, an ox and an eagle (Ezekiel's vision?) representing Matthew, Mark, Luke and John.

Some of the notable people associated with Sherwell include David Derry, who laid the foundation stone, became Mayor, and is remembered in a stained glass window provided by his son, William Derry, the latter being recalled as being not only one of our past Mayors but because of Derry's clock (erected 1862 and still going strong, despite so many changes around it). Also Alfred Rooker, son of the Rev. William Rooker of Tavistock who was mayor at the time of the Guildhall building 1870/1874. Until the blitz a white marble statue on a Cornish granite pedestal of Mr. Rooker stood in the Guildhall square. He had joined Sherwell Church in 1846 and later became senior deacon; his memory is kept alive by a stained glass window.

Other windows of note are:- The Drake window and the Mayflower window. Also existing in the Deacon's vestry is the 1864 model of the church by J. Risdon who was engaged on the construction.

A church well worth a visit, if only to see the outstanding stained glass.

Wycliffe Church, Albert Road.

As noted in connection with Pilgrim Church there were three secessions from the Princes Street, Devonport, Congregational Church. Wycliffe was founded from the second of these in 1808. Services were held alternately in the Pembroke Street and Morice

Square Baptist churches and held in a large room in Granby Street. In 1816 a move was made to Mount Street where a church was built to seat 800. In 1851 a further move was made to the newly built (1850) Temperance Hall (later to become the 'Welcome'). After two years the congregation transferred to the Salem Chapel at the lower end of Albert Road (subsequently to become the Albert Road United Methodist Church) and finally to the top of Albert Road where Wycliffe Congregational Chapel was erected in 1858 on a site adjoining one which was later to become the LSWR rail Halt.

The new chapel was said to be in the Gothic style and had schoolrooms attached. The premises remained until 1941 when it was destroyed by incendiaries, services then continuing in a hut at the rear with a billiard table taking the place of a Communion table. Despite difficulties (it is said that when it rained, the congregation had to use umbrellas) services were maintained until 1950 when Wycliffe and Whitfield merged, to become the present Pilgrim Church. Wycliffe is remembered at Pilgrim by a stone marked:- 'The stone below is part of the Wycliffe Congregational Chapel, Albert Road. Built 1858. Destroyed 1941'.

See also notes on Pilgrim.

Honicknowle United Reformed Church.

In the 1941 blitz, the Union Church (built 1848) situated in Courtenay Street, was destroyed. The war damage compensation provided some of the money to build the Honicknowle Church, much of the pioneering work being carried out by Sherwell. Built in 1957, this is a fair sized brick building facing Honicknowle Green. It appears to have no resident minister but is served from Trinity United Reformed Church in Hartley.
Externally, it seems to be a modern purpose built structure in a modern district.

Western College Congregational Chapel (see also 'General Notes')

Opened in 1861 in the Mannamead/Mutley district. This is no longer used for religious purposes.

Batter Street, Congregational Church.

Built about 1704, this can claim descent from George Hughes, the Puritan vicar of St. Andrews who was ejected from that church in 1662.
Batter Street became the mother church of the Emma Place Congregation Church built in 1787 and of the Union Church in Courtenay Street built in 1848.
Owing to changes of distribution of population attendances at Batter Street decreased at the beginning of this century and it was purchased by Lord Astor in 1923.
It was opened by the Astors in 1925 as the Virginia House Settlement and still continues to serve as a Community Centre. An interesting point on the old Batter Street Church is that Nicholas Sherwell (see also Sherwell U.R. Church) was Minister for some time. In fact, such was the shortage of Ministers, he is said to have served both Batter St. and the Unitarian congregations for about 10 years from 1662? onwards. Noted as having unusual stepped gables.

Congregational - General Notes.

Other places of worship said to have existed as follows:-

Compton	1850/1854	Moon St.	1854
How St.	1886/1889.	Higher Lane.	1866/1871
Claremont St.	1867/1868	James St.	1869/1884
Richmond St.	1878/1880	Deptford Pl.	1881/1890
Laira St.	1867/1868	Clifton St.	1871/1880
Martin Lane, Millbay	1861/1871		

Reference has already been made to the Union Chapel (1848/1941) in Courtenay Street and the Emma Place Chapel, Stonehouse built 1787.

Western College.

A Congregational Ministerial Training Institution was originally formed in Exeter in 1752 and was removed to Plymouth in 1845. The present building erected to the design of Mr. Hine is said to be Modern Gothic. No longer used for religious purposes.

OTHER DENOMINATIONS

The Seventh-day Adventist Church.

The movement began about 1840, a headquarters being established at Battle Creek, Michigan, U.S.A. In 1874 the first Missionary was sent abroad and in 1903 the headquarters moved to Washington. D.C.
The Church was officially organised in Plymouth in 1903 and meetings were held at the Flete Hall in Ebrington Street. A permanent meeting place did not exist until 1919, when premises consisting of two large and one small room were used at 19 Greenbank Avenue (junction of Greenbank Avenue and Beaumont Road).These premises housed both the Church and the School.
In 1929 a large house was acquired in North Road and this was modified by having the Church below and the school above. Contemporary records suggest that at this time there were many shortages but these were overcome and the school thrived, as well as attendances at the Church increasing.
During the war the building escaped damage despite so much devastation in the district.
At the present time, both Church and School prosper having a happy 'family' atmosphere. Many pupils have scattered to various parts of the globe where they maintain and spread the religion.

Jehovah's Witnesses.

Formerly known as International Bible Students, the movement officially adopted the name of Jehovah's Witnesses in 1931.
The group was organised in 1872 by Charles Taze Russell and his successor in leadership was Joseph Franklin Rutherford (Judge Rutherford).
In 1884 there was formed a corporation known as The Watch Tower Bible and Tract Society. The Witnesses use tracts, books, magazines and recordings in making contacts with the public and are well known for their house to house visits. They regard certain other Christian groups as misguided by Satan.
Before the last war, premises at Russell Street, Plymouth, were used and described as the International Bible Students Association Tabernacle. At the present time, meeting places which are known as 'Kingdom Halls' exist at Gordon Terrace (next to the Apostolic Church) and at Keyham.
The number of members in Plymouth is not known but it is said that in the latter 1950s there were 16,000 congregations in the United States and other places.

Plymouth Spiritualist Churches.

From about 1921 onwards, a Spiritualist Church existed in the premises of the Oddfellows' Hall in Morley Street, Plymouth. The Church was closed through flooding and after the war the site of Morley Street was swept away due to city re-planning. The ground is now covered by the lower end of Cornwall Street.
The Ferry Road (Morice Town) Spiritualist Church was in use for about 27 years until the site was absorbed in the post war Dockyard extension. At one time, too, a room had been rented, in the 'Homeward Bound' restaurant at the lower end of Albert Road, Devonport - almost opposite the Dockyard Albert Gate.
The present Brunswick Spiritualist National Church in Keppel Place, Devonport, was opened on 23rd, April, 1955. It was built on

ground formerly occupied by war blitzed dwelling houses. The site is freehold and its construction and formation would not have been possible but for the generous help given by Mrs. Farley and friends from the previously existing Morley Spiritualist Church.

The Brunswick Church seats perhaps 100 persons and besides having an organ, also has a small rostrum which came from the old Ferry Road premises. The building is modern in appearance and partly surrounded by a small well-kept garden. Inside, by the side of the rostrum, the Opening Prayer is noted:- "O Lord, I am in Thy Holy House. Keep my eyes and my thoughts from wandering and help me to worship thee in spirit and in truth. Amen".

From the inception of the Brunswick Church, it is obvious that it owes much to the dedicated work of Mr. and Mrs. Behenna. Mr. Behenna is now dead and Mrs. Behenna has given and is still giving much of her life to the service of the Church, which is now noted as being free from debt.

Daughter churches of Brunswick are at Connaught Avenue and Grimstone Terrace.

Other meeting places of the Spiritualist Movement are said to exist or have existed at the Leigham Hall, West Hoe, Plymouth Psychical Research Institute, North Hill Villa.

Before leaving the details of the Brunswick Spiritualist National Church, it should be noted that it is licenced for the performance of baptisms, marriages and funerals.

Note: The church is reserved for strictly religious purposes only.

General.

It would appear that the modern origin of the Spiritualist Movement started in America in 1848, when Kate Fox, the daughter of a farmer in New York State, as a result of odd disturbances in the house, attempted to establish communication with the spirit of a man who had been murdered there.

The practice of having sittings for communications with spirits spread rapidly from that time. Kate Fox (afterwards Mrs. Fox

Jencken) and one of her sisters gave much of their later lives to acting as mediums in the U.S. and in England. Later the movement became wide spread.

The Spiritualist Movement was formed in1890. The seven principles are:-
(1) The Fatherhood of God.
(2) The Brotherhood of Man.
(3) The Communion of Spirits and the Ministry of Angels.
(4) The Continuous existence of the Human Soul.
(5) Personal responsibility
(6) Compensation and redistribution thereafter for all good or evil deeds done on earth.
(7) Eternal progress open to every human soul.

The Apostolic Church, Gordon Terrace.

In writing about this church, I can do no better than to quote from details supplied by Mr. Leonard Burrell: "How the Movement started. Two brothers, Daniel and Jones Williams living at Pennygroes, near Ammanford, South Wales, were 'born-again' as a result of the 1904-5 Revival.

Later, in 1907-8, these two young men received Baptism in the Spirit as Acts, Chapter 2.

DanWilliams was a miner and he would hold bible talks and prayers during the lunch breaks and it was at this time that he heard the Voice of the Lord calling him to full time work.

Already the brothers were Lay preachers at the Congregational Church but when they and many others were baptised in the Holy Spirit, they left their several churches and commenced meetings (Pentecostal) in their own homes, later acquiring a building at Pennygroes. Soon their eyes were opened to the Holy Spirit to Divine Government, the purpose of God for this dispensation (see Ephesians Ch. 4.1-16). Soon many more Spirit filled Christians from all over the country sought to know more of this Doctrine - soon many bodies joined and the Apostolic Church was reborn.

Local History: By the 1920's, the vision had spread to Cornwall (Porthlevan). Five women from Plymouth went to some of the meetings and realised the truth of the Holy Spirit and Divine Government operating on Earth through Apostles, Prophets, Evangelists, Pastors and Teachers.

One lady and her daughter (Mrs. Mann) living in Grenville Road, Prince Rock, started prayer meetings in her house, praying for the Baptism and for help to commence an Apostolic church in Plymouth.

The fishermen from Newlyn and Porthleven always came to Plymouth at the herring season and stayed for several weeks among the fishermen, some of whom had embraced the Apostolic belief and many joined in the Grenville Road meetings. There were five women and a few men interested. The ladies, after months of prayer, were led by the Lord to a large room in Vauxhall Street on premises then occupied by a firm of Engineers name Little.

The South West was at that time controlled from Hereford and it was from here that Ministry and soon a full time Pastor was sent to Plymouth. This would be in the 1931-32 period.

Moves were made to many other locations (no doubt due to the disruption caused by the blitz) until 1952, when local men and women, under the supervision of Pastor Hugh Dawson (President of the Council at that time) built the present premises in Gordon Terrace. This new Church was opened on 18th April, 1953. Plymouth now comes under the Porthleven area, and in this district Apostolic Churches now exist at Barnstaple, Exeter, Redruth, Porthleven, Carleen, and Newlyn".

The above details are quoted almost word for word.

I am indebted to Pastor Cawthorne and Mr. Burrell for their kindness in supplying this information.

The present church is unique in construction. Designed by a Pastor of the Apostolic faith who was an architect, it appears to have been a community effort by members of the congregation.

Steel frames to form curved slabs made by another pastor who had been a blacksmith.

Method of erection was to put frames in place, cover with hessian, form the curved arch-like slabs with 2" concrete and when this was set, to remove frame and form another portion. Gradually the length of the church was formed and although from the outside the building looks like a concrete Nissen hut, it has been squared inside to make an attractive building. Designed with view to enable the church to be easy of access to the disabled a point frequently forgotten in more elaborate structures. The construction of this unusual church says much for the skill and devotion of the congregation.

The Bethel Mission, Barbican.

In 1820, the Plymouth, Plymouth Dock and Stonehouse Soldiers and Seamen's Friendly Society and Bethel Union was formed and a loft was hired close to the Fishermens' Steps, Barbican. 54 men and 24 boys are said to have attended twice each Sunday to receive religious instruction and to learn to read and write. The number of those attending soon grew and although the loft would hold 200 persons, it became too small. In 1832 a block of buildings were erected near the Mayflower Stone and later some classrooms were added.

A new building (the present one) was erected in 1883 at the lower end of Castle St. (sometimes known as Damnation Alley, which in 1850 had been noted as having 7 public houses and five beer houses - a contemporary comment being:- ".... every house was an inn and every inn a brothel ....").

The new building became known as The Seamen's Bethel and in the early days was largely supported by Methodists and Independent churches, although Ministers of other different denominations served also. It had great influence in the area, even at one time stopping Sunday fishing. It existed mainly to provide for the spiritual and bodily needs of fishermen, soldiers and sailors of the district (the Citadel and Elphinstone Barracks were nearby). One wedding only has been celebrated at the Mission and this was in 1950.

Formerly known as the Seaman's Bethel, now as the Bethel Mission, it still fulfils a need in an area which has seen so many changes.

The Brethren (Plymouth Brethren).

At a meeting in Dublin in 1825 attended by J.N. Darby, A.N. Groves (a former Plymouth dentist), E. Cronin and Lord Congleton, the Brethren came into being. Darby, a curate in County Wicklow, then left the church.

Darby was invited to preach in Plymouth and the effect was said to have been immediate. Meetings were held in private houses until such time as a proper chapel could be erected. A site was purchased in Raleigh Street and a building (believed to have been designed by John Foulston) erected thereon. It was known by several names:- The Temperance Hall, The Raleigh Street Chapel, Providence Chapel, and was the first permanent meeting place for the Brethren to be built in England. Another account says:- 'A wealthy man, G.W. Wigram, came to Plymouth and provided the means for the origin of the Plymouth Meeting; in 1831 he bought the recently completed Providence Chapel in Raleigh Street for £750, which for some reason was not needed for its original purpose'.

Services began in 1832 and when the accommodation became inadequate, the main services were transferred to the Ebrington Street Chapel in 1840. Another version of this is that Darby disagreed with a certain book and built the chapel in Ebrington Street in 1845. This building was said to have held 1,000 persons and was very plain in appearance. It is described by A.N. Harris, FRAS in 1911 as follows:- ".... I never knew who was the architect of the Brethren but he succeeded in producing something unlike anything in heaven above, or in the earth beneath. It was named 'The Dutch Oven' (by outsiders, in derision to which it had a resemblance). The large flat side of it was towards Ebrington Street with several smaller flat surfaces arranged in a semicircle behind; there were two entrances in Ebrington Street a few feet from the ends of the building, and a row of plain windows above, two rows of windows upper and lower extended around the rest of the building. On the inside not a vestige of ornament could be seen but the place was comfortable and the seats admirably arranged. Each person could see and hear well, the tiers of seats arranged in a semicircle being well above each other, well warmed and well lighted".

The writer went on to say:- ".... after the rupture, the large building ceased to be used and a consignment of Brethren met in the Raleigh Hall, the rest were glad of any large room available .... proposed that a building be erected for the purpose of uniting some of the smaller parties .... a site obtained in Compton Street and a suitable building soon appeared (here the name of OLDFORD is mentioned. W.J.P.) .... the chapel is now turned into a paint store for Messrs Widger & Co. A goodly number used to meet in a large room in Union Street .... the place is now used as a long drinking bar". End of 1911 extract.

It would appear from the above that after leaving Ebrington Street, the main body of Brethren went to Raleigh Street in 1848. The Ebrington St. premises were taken over by the Wesleyans about 1857, rebuilt in 1897, gutted by fire in 1937 (when its use for religious purposes ended), partly restored and used as a restaurant, and demolished in the 1950's. It certainly seems to have been a site with an interesting history.

Back to the Brethren. In 1908, one testimony only existed at Raleigh Street (now a short street at the rear of the Co-operative Building). Eight couples came from Devonport to attend the meetings.

Lambert Hall in a street off Fore Street, Devonport, was used and in 1909 a large room over a shop in Albert Road was rented (this became known as the Albert Hall). So it seems at that time we have: Raleigh Street, Lambert Street and the Albert Hall and this was the position until the outbreak of the 1914/1918 war when the Lambert Street premises were requisitioned for military purposes. By 1921, numbers in excess of 100 were attending the Albert Hall and the overcrowding was so great that is was sometimes necessary for the Brethren to sit on the stairs. It was decided that new premises were necessary; a site was secured in Wolseley Road and a wood and asbestos building erected. Services began here and it was in constant use and although badly damaged in the blitz, religious observances were able to be continued, temporary repairs having been made. Due to the deterioration of the fabric of the hall, however, it was decided that a permanent structure should be erected. This project was put in hand about 1961 and in 1962 the new brick built premises (now known as the Gospel Hall) were opened. At the opening ceremony, a short talk (from which some of these notes are made) was given by Mr. Bishop dealing with the history of the Brethren in Plymouth and Devonport. The 'temporary' wooden hut had lasted 43 years.

At the present time (1977), the Gospel Hall is in full use. Apart from the normal regular meetings of Testimony and the breaking of bread, weddings are celebrated and funerals take place. Adjoining rooms are used for social and other activities.

It should be mentioned here that the Providence Chapel in Raleigh Street escaped the blitz but was demolished in the course of City re-planning and reconstruction.

In addition to the above, premises used by the Open Brethren also exist at Ford Park (this is really the main church) and took the place of Raleigh Street, Whitleigh, West Hill (close to Freedom Fields), Plymstock, Plympton and on at Burraton, Saltash, the last named being an offshoot of the Gospel Hall in Wolseley Road.

The Exclusive Brethren, The Exclusive's have very rigid rules. Premises are at Lucas Terrace and at Hender's Corner (near Mannamead).

In these notes, due to the many splits and secessions, it has not been possible in a short space to give anything other than a general account, and although efforts have been made to get the facts right, some errors will doubtless have crept in.

Church of Christ, Scientist.

It is not possible to talk of this Church without reference to Mary Baker Eddy. Born in 1821 in Hampshire, she was a deeply religious person, and her reading of Matthew 9, 2-8 led to her recovery from an accident and the discovery in the Bible of the scientific law which underlay the healing works of Christ.
She discussed her beliefs with others and began to take students, as well as publishing 'Science and Health' in 1875.
The first formal steps taken to organise the Church were taken in 1879; meetings were first held in rented halls, but in 1895 the Mother Church was dedicated and is now, with the imposing extension of 1906, one of Boston's landmarks.
In Plymouth, as far back as 1903, a Naval Officer received healing through Christian Science and getting in touch with others of similar interests, a little group was started and meetings took place in a private house in Ford Park Road (almost opposite the present church). Meetings were held here for 2½ years.
In 1906, due to increasing numbers, rooms 38-40 in the Sun Buildings (Spooner's Corner opposite St. Andrew's) were rented. A Sunday School was started in 1907, followed by the acquisition of larger premises in Ebrington Street in 1909 for religious services.
In 1912 a house (No. 12 Treville Street) was taken and this acted as a church, Sunday School and Reading Room. Later, during the First World War, war relief rooms were opened in Union Street.
A wooden building was erected on a site in Ford Park Road in 1920, and after recognition as 'The First Church of Christ, Scientist, Plymouth' in 1922, this temporary building was dedicated in 1924.
It became obvious that a permanent church should be built and to this end a foundation stone was laid in 1930. This was completed in

part during the following year and was used until 1938 when it was decided not to carry out any more work on this, but to construct an entirely new church on the site of the old wooden building, then being used as a Sunday School.

Plans for the new structure went ahead and in 1939 the foundation stone of the present church was laid and the new building completed in 1940. The war years followed and a rest room for the forces was maintained in Tavistock Road 1942/1945.

Happily, the new church in Ford Park Road remained undamaged during the blitz (Mutley being one of the few main areas of Plymouth which was largely untouched) and the building was dedicated in 1948.

Externally, this is a pleasant red brick building in excellent surroundings and fronted with a few small trees. Internally it is well lighted by large windows by day and by concealed lighting at night. It has an excellent electronic organ, the musical reproduction of which is said to be outstanding. Reading rooms and other rooms are attached and the whole group of buildings form an excellent addition to a busy area, besides serving the religious needs of so many people.

P.S. It is also noted that three rooms in Westwell Park Chambers, Westwell St., were used by the Christian Science Society during the pre-war period.

The Christadelphian Ecclesia, Portland Villas, Plymouth.

The Christadelphians (Brethren of Christ) sometimes also called the 'Thomasites' were founded by John Thomas (1805-1871). He studied medicine in London and in 1844 migrated to Brooklyn, N.Y. Here he founded a religious sect about 1848, which became organised and known as the Christadelphians during the Civil War. The Bible is considered the only authoritative creed and membership of the Society required a profession of faith and baptism by total immersion.

Locally, an Ecclesia was formed in Devonport in 1868 and from that time occupied various buildings in and around Plymouth, before moving to the present location in 1965. The building now used was formerly a Salvation Army H.Q. but was relinquished by the Army when they moved to new premises in Armada Way. There are many Christadelphian Ecclesias throughout the world, all run independently but sharing the same beliefs. To quote from an explanatory booklet:- "…. is circulated with a view to helping you share in the same faith and hope and to prepare for the return of the Lord Jesus Christ, the nearness of which event is plainly discernible in the many signs to be seen in the political heavens, as well as in the social and religious world".

The Elim Church, Notte Street.

The present building is on the site of the former Cookworthy Mansion, parts of which still appear to remain. A tablet commemorates his occupancy and reads:-
"WILLIAM COOKWORTHY 1705-1780. CHEMIST AND POTTER, DWELT FOR MANY YEARS IN A HOUSE ON THIS SITE. HE WAS THE MAKER OF PLYMOUTH CHINA, THE FIRST TRUE ENGLISH PORCELAIN".
Cookworthy was a notable Quaker and when in residence it is known that Captain Cook was a visitor and that John Smeaton stayed there for at least some of the time during the construction of the Eddystone Lighthouse. Old photos show that it was later converted into two houses and it is noteworthy that the pediments over the windows of the present church appear identical with the one shown over the doorway of the original building. The firm of Cookworthy and Beavan later became Balkwill's, Chemists - a firm well remembered by many Plymothians. The house was rebuilt in 1883.
The building was purchased by Isaac Foot, who, when Mayor of Plymouth, used it as a Mayoralty House. Later he built a Methodist Mission on the site, which was subsequently superintended by his

son, the Rt.Hon. Isaac Foot, father of the famous family of politicians.

The Mission building was bombed during the last war, only the shell remaining. The site was sold to the Elim congregation on the understanding that the frontage on Notte Street should remain unchanged.

Elim here in Plymouth was founded in 1924, first meeting in a disused foundry (Willoughby's possibly) and known as the Elim Tabernacle. After the last war the Congregation Church in Emma Place was acquired and when the lease ran out the present premises in Notte Street were purchased, as noted above.

The interior was completely restructured to form the existing church which will now hold 300 worshippers. It contains an organ of some value which had originally been installed in the Zion Methodist Church, Torquay. Over the platform at the front of the church are the words:- "I KNOW THAT MY REDEEMER LIVETH" and in the vestry is a poem hung on the wall which gives the history in rhyme.

The Elim Church is well attended and serves the district well.

Plymouth Friends (Quakers).

A Christian body, formed in the middle of the 17th century, and although the Toleration Act of 1869 did much to relieve religious persecution, the Quakers suffered much and their conscientious beliefs frequently brought them in conflict with the law.

In 1654, John Audland and Thomas Arey came to Plymouth to teach Christianity. They were followers of James Fox, who held that guidance should come from God alone, not from Ministers or priests. In the next year, Fox himself visited the town and was later imprisoned at Launceston. The early Friends were very militant and were frequently badly handled.

The name 'Quaker' comes from those days of oppression. George Fox was before the magistrates in 1650 and he bade the Judge "to quake at the name of the Lord". As has been mentioned, the movement was originally very militant in furtherance of its beliefs, and a contemporary report notes that at one of the Plymouth meetings of George Fox ".... came in some jangling Baptists, but the Lord's power overcame them" - it is not known what form the Lord's power took!!

The first meeting place was established in a thatched house in Sussex St., the property of John Harris of Pennycross and this was probably used continuously until the opening of larger premises at Bilbury (Treville) St. in 1674. These premises consisted of two large houses which had been purchased and suitably converted.

In 1804 the old building which had served for thirty years was rebuilt on the same site, the Meeting House then constructed remaining until about 1950. In addition, about 1899 another meeting place had been established on Mutley Plain this being the first building on this site.

Treville St. premises continued to be used by the Friends until 1920 when a new Settlement was established in enlarged premises at Mutley Plain. Between 1920 and 1950 the old building in Treville St. had become Plymouth's main Labour Exchange, but was demolished about 1950 to make way for the new Bus Station. At this time, the graveyard at the site of the old meeting house (containing the remains of Cookworthy, the famous Chemist) was disturbed and the bones re-interred at Efford.

Swarthmore Settlement now takes a firm part in the social and cultural activities of the City, besides performing its main function as a religious meeting place. The Settlement is well known for its pleasant and friendly atmosphere - truly a Society of Friends.

The Church of Jesus Christ of the Latter Day Saints (Mormons)

The Movement was started in the United States by Joseph Smith (1805-1844), the first church being founded in Fayette in 1830. As early as 1840 the religion came to England and it was probably shortly after this that a meeting place was established at Eldad, in fact, before the creation of the Parish of St. Peter in 1843, this was the only chapel in the area. Other meeting places are said to have existed at the Odd Fellows Lodge Room, Willow Plot (1852) bottom of Ker Street, adjoining 74, George St., Devonport (1856), at the 'Billiard Room', Pembroke St., Devonport (1864), and at a large room on the ground floor of 32, College Road, Mannamead (1936). It is not known how accurate the bracketed dates are quoted in this paragraph. It appears that for some years there was no representation in Plymouth as it is believed Mormons had been encouraged to emigrate.

The present Plymouth church was built on the site of 'Inceworth', previously owned by Dr. Innes. Work started about 1964 under the supervision of Carl Spencer, who had come over from Arizona with his wife and two children.

The architect of the new church was British and the land on which it stands cost £68,000. The building of the new structure was not without incident as, on one occasion some tar on the roof caught alight, causing the explosion of two gas cylinders. Those engaged on the roof jumped off and although some damage resulted, there was no loss of life.

During construction an old well was discovered (this can still be seen). The work took two years to complete, much of the labour being done voluntarily by church members. When the building was complete, Mr. Spencer and his family returned to the States.

The church was opened about 1966 but as a large debt still remained, the dedication was not carried out until this had been cleared off. Dedication two years later was by Elder Cullimore, an Assistant to the quorum of 12 Apostles.

The Church of the Latter Day Saints is very modern in appearance and constructed of a reddish brown brick. It has a small tower over the main entrances and is situated amid sweeping lawns and fine trees. Besides its function for religious observance, the building contains extensive accommodation for social and recreational activities.

An unusual but attractive building which certainly enhances the district.

The Salvation Army.

In 1865, the Rev. William Booth commenced his ministry in East London and in 1867 the first H.Q. was opened in Whitechapel. The Christian Mission became the Salvation Army in 1878 and brass bands were introduced into the movement.
William Booth died in 1912 and his son, Bramwell Booth was promoted to General. He died in 1929.
In Plymouth the 1st Corps was founded in 1878 by Captain J. Dowdle and soon after the Congress Hall was opened in Martin St. near the Octagon. It is understood that this Hall was built for the Army by Isaac Foot.
Many other premises in Plymouth and Devonport are or have been used in the past. These include:-
  Granby Street, Devonport (S.A Barracks)
  College Road.Keyham (previously Primitive Methodist Chapel)
  St. Budeaux
  How Street (Salvation Army Barracks)
  Gloucester Street, Morice Town
  Ross Street, Devonport (room in the Old Malt House)
  Farringdon Road
  Mount Street, Devonport (doubtful)
  Crownhill (S.A Hall)
Early Salvation Army places of worship still known to exist are the Shaftesbury Hall in Deptford Place (this is a red brick building with a little square tower. Its age is not known but adjacent Shaftesbury Cottages are dated 1861), and the Congress Hall in Exeter Street. The 'War Cry' of October 17th, 1936, gave a full page of pictures headed:- "Celebrating fifty eight years Fighting at the Plymouth Congress Hall" and the photos show Major Herbert Horsley, the C.O, the Senior Band under the leadership of Leslie Burgoyne, Mrs. Major Horsley, the Singing Company (Leader: Margaret Eke), the Corps Cadet Brigade (Guardian: Lila Leah), The Songsters (Leader: Alfred Hayter), Members of the Senior Census Board, Young Peoples' Legion (Leader: Mrs. Weymouth), S/M Mrs.

Crocker, The Concertina Band (Leader: Winifred Tucker, ALCM), The Chum Brigade (Leader: Norman Rogers), The Young People Workers, The Life Saving Guards (Leader: Beatrice Harris), The Sunbeams (Leader: Mrs. Otter), Members of the Home League, a group of Veterans with over 1,000 years' service, The Young Peoples' Band, and the Cycle Brigade who are noted as being Evangelists for the villages. These details have been included as they may bring back memories to old Salvationists.

The Congress Hall in Martin St. was destroyed in the blitz. After the bombing, a gift of £9,500 was made by the citizens and Salvationists of Plymouth, U.S.A., a charitable and sympathetic gesture which should not be forgotten - one of the many acts of goodwill from the United States which were so appreciated in those dark days.

Temporary accommodation was found at Portland Villas (premises now used by the Christadelphians) until a fine new Headquarters was built in Armada Way. This was opened in 1960 by General Wilfred Kitching almost 30 years after the destruction of the original H.Q. A plaque in the entrance hall reads:- "This new Congress Hall was erected 1959-1960 to replace the original Congress Hall in Martin Street which was destroyed during the World War 1939-1945".

The new Congress Hall in Armada Way is a fine, large building which has been constructed to match the surrounding shops and places of business. Internally it has a large platform and ample seating accommodation is provided in the body of the hall and in the extensive gallery.

Members of the Army do untold good work among the poor and in times of national need (many will remember their war time service). They are sometimes smiled at, yet they are universally respected and liked for their dedicated service.

Much of the information came from Mr. T. Tabb of Plymouth, who was born in 1900 and has been a Salvationist all his life. His service has mainly taken place in the band, his instrument being the cornet.

The Seventh-day Adventists Church.

In 1855 a headquarters was established at Battle Creek, Michigan, USA, and a formal denominational organisation created. In 1874 the first Missionary was sent abroad and in 1903 the headquarters moved to Washington.

The church was officially organised in Plymouth in 1903 and meetings were held at the Flete Hall in Ebrington St. A permanent meeting place did not exist until 1919, when premises consisting of two large and one small room were used at 19, Greenbank Avenue (junction of Greenbank Ave and Beaumont Road). These premises housed both the Church and the school, both of which are closely connected.

In 1929 a large house was acquired in North Road. This was modified by having the Church in the lower section and the school above. Contemporary records suggest that at this time there were many shortages but these were overcome and both the church and the school thrived.

During the war the building escaped damage, despite much devastation in the vicinity.

At present time, both the church and the school prosper - the school having a happy 'family' atmosphere. Many past pupils have scattered to various parts of the globe where they maintain and spread the religion.

The Synagogue, Catherine Street.

By the end of the 17th century there was a number of Jews who resided permanently in Plymouth. The Jewish community increased and regular services were held in private houses. The need for a permanent building became apparent and to this end proceedings were started in 1742 to build a synagogue. At that time, Jews were not allowed to own land but a plot of ground was obtained on lease by George Marshall, Snr, who acted on behalf of the founders, the cost of the leased ground being 5/- per year.

In 1762 a Synagogue was built, essentially in its present form, the nominal holder of the lease at that time being Samuel Champion. In 1797 it became possible for Jews to own property and in that year a lease for 99 years was obtained on behalf of the congregation. This was converted to freehold in 1834. Ground for the vestry was bought in 1873 and this was erected in the following year. One account says that when the Guildhall was constructed 1870-1874, a piece of ground was taken from the Jews and that they were given a bit of the old workhouse site to build the vestry on in exchange.

The only major alteration to the Synagogue since it was built in 1762 was the extension to the Ladies Gallery carried out in 1864. It is said that the ritual slaughterer of animals in Plymouth, Michael Alexander, became a Christian and was baptised at nearby St. Andrew's, subsequently becoming the first Anglican Bishop of Jerusalem.

During the last war, despite extensive damage in the vicinity, the Synagogue escaped and amid so much havoc this was outstanding. It was at this time that the Jews extended their hospitality to the Unitarians, whose own premises had been destroyed. For some weeks they were permitted to use part of the premises on Sunday afternoons - a truly charitable gesture.

At one time a Synagogue existed in Devonport on a site (now absorbed by the Dockyard) directly opposite St. Aubyn Church at 66, Chapel St.

The Plymouth Synagogue is in a quiet spot and must be unknown to many Plymothians. Situated just below the City Treasury (one time Police Station) in Catherine Street, it is approached by a narrow lane. From the outside the building is very plain although some stained glass can be seen, the beauty of which is not revealed unless viewed from inside. One window depicts a pair of scales and ram's horns, this being associated with Abraham's devotion to the Lord when he was prepared to sacrifice his own son. As will be remembered, a ram was found caught in some nearby bushes and

slaughtered instead. It is understood that the ceremonial ram's Horn is sounded to mark the commencement of the Jewish New Year.
The interior of the Synagogue is reached through an oak panelled vestibule and on entering one is struck by the central platform surrounded by eight brass candlesticks. The focal point is, of course, the Ark which contains the Sacred Scrolls and above the Ark can be seen the Tablets of the Ten Commandments.
The gallery which runs around three sides of the building is supported by slender pillars and one does find the whole interior to be most unusual but very attractive.
A visit to the Synagogue is an unique experience.

Unitarian Church, Plymouth.

In 1662, in the days of religious intolerance, the Rev. George Hughes who had been vicar of St. Andrew's for 18 years, was ejected from this church because of his non-conformist views. Together with other clergymen, one of whom was Nicholas Sherwell, the congregations of Batter Street and Treville Street arose. Before the foundations of these two communities however, secret meetings were held in barns and in private houses.
The first authorised place of worship appears to have been at Green House in Green Street (near Charles Church). In the last few years of the 17th century, the congregation met at a house in Bilbury St. (later Treville St.) and in 1700 the first meeting house was built. Meetings were also held at Batter St. but these were more orthodox in character. Treville St. became Unitarian, and Batter St. Independent. The original building in Treville St. was becoming dilapidated, was demolished and a new imposing structure erected in 1831. The first minister was the Rev. W.J. Odgers, a person of some note who, together with ministers from nearby St. Andrew's, had much to do with the cleaning up and welfare of the Barbican area.
The Treville St. church, which many still remember, was destroyed

in the 1941 blitz, one of the 42 churches in the Plymouth area to suffer this fate. Its interior had been fairly plain, with a wooden pulpit approached by a small staircase.

After the destruction of the building, for a few weeks the Hebrew Congregation from the nearby Synagogue extended their hospitality to the homeless Unitarians, permitting the use of part of their premises on Sunday afternoons. Later, services were held at a private house in Thorn Park.

In 1943 part of a house in Houndiscombe Road was used, one large room providing accommodation for 35 persons, and two smaller rooms giving facilities for the committee and as a youth club.

The Houndiscombe Road premises were inadequate for the demands made on them, but this was solved when Plymouth Corporation made a compulsory purchase order on the old Treville St. site and the War Damage Commission approved the formulating of plans for a new church.

A site was obtained in Notte Street and plans approved for the new church. Designed by Messrs. Louis de Soisson, it takes the form of a squarish building with a slender tower and spire, an unusual but picturesque addition to the neighbourhood.

Originally it had to serve as both a church and a hall, arrangements existing enabled the front part of the church containing the organ and pulpit to be curtained off. The new building was opened by the Rt. Hon. Chuter Ede in 1958, and so again, after 17 years, the Unitarians had permanent premises. A church hall was added some years later, this being opened by Lord Sorensen in 1966.

A limestone tablet from the Treville St. Church (the site of which is now partly covered by the Bus Station) is built into the side of the new structure. It reads:- "UNITARIAN CHAPEL 1831"- it is nice to think that a bit of the old is incorporated in the new.

The interior of the present church is modern and pleasant, the outstanding feature being the mural facing the congregation. It depicts Christ stilling the waves on the Sea of Galilee: 'Lord, save us or we perish'.

Unitarian Churches in Devonport.

At the top of Duke Street and facing Cumberland Gardens is a public house known as 'The Old Chapel'. This was, in fact, the first Unitarian Church in Devonport.
Open on 27th April, 1791, as a Unitarian place of worship - much help having been received by the Plymouth Minister, the Rev. Thomas Porter - it prospered for a time, but due to persecution and religious intolerance, the congregation became negligible. An example of such intolerance was that the then Controller of the Dockyard announced that he considered that all persons attending the church to be disloyal subjects and would be discharged. This official opposition had the effect of intimidating many workers, professional men and tradesmen also withdrawing their support. One wonders how sincere the Commissioner was, as in 1816 he sold a plot of land for the erection of the Ebenezer Church (now Plymouth Central Hall).
Despite valiant efforts of several clergymen, the Devonport Chapel had to close and was sold in 1806.
Times changed and mainly due to the tolerance of a newcomer to the town, a Mr. Gibbs, who occupied a responsible position in the Dockyard, a new Unitarian group was formed, meeting occasionally in a hired room for lectures and services. Interest grew, so much so that a new Chapel was opened in Granby St. in 1829. This was probably not a very elaborate building but it did hold 270 persons and was in use for at least 35 years. Membership increased so much that in 1866 a fine new building was erected in Duke St. This was cited almost opposite the church of St John and was named Christ Church. Designed by Mr. Alfred Norman it is said to have been in the Gothic style and had a gallery for organ as well as a vestry and classrooms. Some of the windows are reported to have been of richly stained glass.
The congregation of Christ Church declined during the 1914/18 war and the building was closed. In 1923 it was sold to the Y.M.C.A. who used it as a gymnasium. Later the Y.M.C.A. moved

to Fore St. to premises also being used by the Electric Cinema (the old Devonport Public Hall).

It is remembered that the old church stood empty for some years and that it is believed to have survived the blitz, only to be acquired by compulsory purchase and demolished. The site was included in the Dockyard extension and is just inside the wall opposite the Library.

Finally, the 'Old Chapel' Public House still remains; what was the crypt now thought to be used as a bar and restaurant. A point of interest is that until 1957 it was not allowed to open on Sundays (in deference to its religious origins?). One of the most interesting buildings in Devonport, and other than St Aubyn Parish Church (1772), must be one of the oldest.

Devonport Town Mission, Granby Street (Zion)

Not by any means the largest church in Plymouth but one with a fascinating history. Perhaps we can do no better than to start with a quote from the notes of Miss May Uglow, who probably more than any one person, was associated with Zion in the early days:

"In the year 1863 Devonport Town Mission was started. A number of gentlemen appointed one man of evangelical principles and personal purity.

1867. Money needed and on March 18th the first meeting of the Ladies Committee was held to appoint collectors and raise money. That year allowed the appointment of another man.

1867. In September, too, two teaching places were opened, one in Moon's Cove, then called, I believe, Mounts Cove; another in Albert Road in the Missioner's house.

1875. A third Missioner was appointed and this time a lady - a Miss Hollock, and two years afterwards, a second female - a Miss Foale.

1886. Two more places for preaching were opened: one in Geake's Alley, Devonport, and a room in Cornwall Street, Devonport, and also one in Belmont, Stoke.

1889. Miss Pinhay was appointed, the first female missionary having died and two women missioners carried on the work.
1901. Miss Foale resigned and Miss Hopkins was appointed.
1902. Miss Pinhay resigned and Mrs Dennis appointed. In midsummer 1903 new premises were obtained."

The above is a copy of Miss Uglow's notes in her own handwriting and gives something of the origin of Devonport Town Mission, but Miss Uglow herself deserves special mention. She was born in 1884 and started her missionary work at the age of 23. She gave 63 years of her life in dedicated service to the community and died in 1970 at the age of 86. A Memorial Service was held at the Royal Sailors' Rest and instead of a conventional memorial, it was decided to build the Manse adjoining the Mission in Granby Street - a practical gesture and one which is certain that Miss Uglow herself would have approved.

May Uglow became the Missioner in 1907 when conditions in Devonport were bad. The Cornwall Street area was a rough one - a place of some squalor with several Public Houses and frequented by prostitutes, the latter being attracted by the Army and Navy garrisons (Raglan and Granby Barracks and the Royal Naval Barracks). Miss Uglow, whose parents had destined her to become a school teacher, lived in Albert Road and attended the Wycliffe Congregational Church (q.v.). However, she noticed the drunkenness existing and the misery it caused. She rented a loft over a stable (in Wide Lane at the back of Cornwall St. and abutting on the dockyard wall) just above Cornwall Beach and this was furnished with forms to provide a meeting place. She would enter public houses and on finding a woman the worse for drink, take her to the Mission and place her on a form until she recovered her senses. She would try to show the foolishness of drinking and her efforts met with some success.

At the first meeting at the new Mission she is said to have had three people there and on greeting them and enquiring how they were, she was told:- "None the better for your asking". She persevered and would go into public houses (there were two in the immediate vicinity of the Mission - the Ferry Boat and the Swan of Avon) and in this she was helped by a Mr. Thomas. He would play the cornet to attract the drinkers to the Mission but the publicans are said to have countered by playing a gramophone to drown the cornet playing. Mr. Thomas and Miss Uglow are reputed to have stood their ground and eventually the gramophone playing stopped. She was undoubtedly a person of great courage. On one occasion a Mr. Luke, a boot repairer of Queen St. was ill. He was said to have been bad tempered and foul mouthed and many avoided him. Miss Uglow, on hearing of his illness, decided to see him, although her family, possible fearing for her safety, tried to dissuade her. She did go, however, and talk to him. When he recovered he surprised his family by telling them that he was going to the Mission not, as he said, that he was becoming converted but to thank Miss Uglow. We can assume that he was impressed by her sincerity as he did join the congregation and became a devout Christian. This was told me by his daughter who is now living at Prince Rock.

On another occasion the Committee asked her to wear a cloak and bonnet, hoping these would afford her some protection in a rough district. This she did not want to do, saying: "The Lord will protect me". She did, however, wear these items - perhaps just to please the Committee.

When the Cornwall St. Mission was full a cart was placed outside to enable others to take part in the service and in 1910 these premises were enlarged. In 1928 a move was made to Granby Street. The building (the present one) is believed to have been erected as a Congregational Chapel when Congregationalists built a new church at the junction of Princes St. Ope (now High Street) and Princes St. (see notes on Sherwell and Pilgrim).

The vacated premises were subsequently occupied by the Freemasons, who later left to take over their new premises at Stoke. The empty building was acquired by Zion at a cost of £600.

Notable past members of the Mission were: J.B. Love (Jimmy Love to the older Devonport people whose drapery establishment in

Catherine St. was well known), Dr Rollaston, Dr Pullin and Dr Fleming.

At present, Zion Evangelical church is known as Devonport Town Mission and apart from religious observances, also has social activities. Much work is done among the young and it exerts a beneficial influence in the neighbourhood.

Throughout time, our history has been enriched by the work of great women; some are well known such as Florence Nightingale, Nurse Edith Cavell and this city's Lady Astor. The work of May Uglow deserves not to be forgotten.

I am indebted to Pastor Alec Passmore, Miss W. Ash, Mr. & Mrs. Selleck and Mr. & Mrs. Dawe for the help given me to compile this short account.

Lower Street Mission.

This is a square, angular building in limestone and is situated just off Exeter St. near the entrance to the old 'Horsewash'.

Embodied in the structure is a tablet which reads:-
'LOWER STREET BAPTIST MISSION ROOM AND SUNDAY SCHOOL, ESTABLISHED 1849', and at the apex of the gable:- 'ERECTED 1882'.

It is assumed that the 1849 Mission was superseded by the present 1882 structure on the same site.

The Moravian Chapel, James Street, Devonport.

This was situated in James St. almost opposite the Church of St. Mary. The chapel was built in 1771 and rebuilt in 1844. Closed by the Moravians about 1916, it was then taken over by the Loyal Orange Institution of England and renamed the Orange Free Church and was subsequently used until 1953 by members of the Apostolic Church (q.v).

The hall would seat perhaps 200. Had a gallery at the rear (street side) and a high platform on which was an even higher pulpit

The building survived the war but was demolished about 1960, when so much reconstruction went on in that part of the town.

The Hydesville Institute.

This was a fairly modern building at the top of Cannon St., Devonport. Its use was noted 'for Full Gospel Mission' but it is not known how long it was used for religious purposes.
Probably built between the two wars in the 1930's, its post second World War use is remembered as a warehouse.

Zoar Mission, Devonport.

Nothing known except that it existed in the Edinburgh Road district of Devonport, near Fore Street.

© W.J. Power. 1977